Virtue, Valor, & Vanity

Also by Eric Burns

THE AUTOGRAPH:
A Modern Fable of a Father and Daughter

BROADCAST BLUES:
Dispatches from the Twenty-Year War
between a Television Reporter and His Medium

INFAMOUS SCRIBBLERS:
The Founding Fathers and the Rowdy Beginnings
of American Journalism

THE JOY OF BOOKS:
Confessions of a Lifelong Reader

THE SMOKE OF THE GODS:
A Social History of Tobacco

THE SPIRITS OF AMERICA:
A Social History of Alcohol

Virtue, Valor, & Vanity

The Founding Fathers and the Pursuit of Fame

ERIC BURNS

Arcade Publishing • New York

FIRST EDITION

Library of Congress Cataloging-in-Publication Data

Burns, Eric.
  Virtue, valor, and vanity : the Founding Fathers and the pursuit of fame / Eric Burns. —1st ed.
      p. cm.
  Includes bibliographical references and index.
  ISBN 978-1-55970-858-6 (alk. paper)
  1. Founding Fathers of the United States—Biography. 2. United States—Politics and government—1775–1783. 3. United States—Politics and government—1783–1789. 4. Virtue—Political aspects—United States—History—18th century. 5. Courage—Political aspects—United States—History—18th century. 6. Pride and vanity—Political aspects—United States—History—18th century. 7. Fame—Political aspects—United States—History—18th century. I. Title.

  E302.5.B87 2007
  973.3—dc22   2007022841

Published in the United States by Arcade Publishing, Inc., New York
Distributed by Hachette Book Group USA

Visit our Web site at www.arcadepub.com

10 9 8 7 6 5 4 3 2 1

Designed by API

EB

PRINTED IN THE UNITED STATES OF AMERICA

To Gerald E. Murray
whose poetry and courage are unsurpassed

CONTENTS

Introduction
The Crew of the Concord

*H*E WAS NOT THE FIRST ENGLISHMAN to see the New World, but he was one of the first to describe it in detail, to record his impressions as meticulously as if his concern had been history no less than exploration, and to preserve those impressions for all who followed. He wrote of the "many pleasant Islands" before him and of a coastline rocky and irregular. He wrote of forests and streams, trees and plants, wildlife and even wilder human beings, whom he regarded for the most part as benign but referred to as "Savages." He wrote of prospects so pleasing in "the Northern Parts of this Country" that the captain of his ship "did not trouble himself to undertake the discovery of the Southern."

His name was Gabriel Archer, and he set sail from Falmouth, England, on the *Concord* on March 26, 1602. According to one account he was accompanied by thirty-one other men, according to another by twenty-two; both accounts tell us that some of the men planned to stay behind, to settle in the New World and set up trading posts. They did not know where they would build them, what they would trade, or even who their trading partners would be. They were men seeking adventure in a faraway part of the globe. They would deal with specifics later.

The *Concord* arrived somewhere in Maine or Massachusetts, still known then as Virginia, on May 14. Before reaching the mainland, Archer and his mates, under the command of Bartholomew Gosnold, drifted past several of those pleasant islands, which were "for the most part uninhabited, and yet by their fruitfulness capable of maintaining a great number of People."

In fact, the islands did maintain a great number of people, and it didn't take the Englishmen long to meet them and find them like none they had ever seen before. "Their Commander . . . came boldly on board the Ship," Archer wrote. "The Commander himself was dress'd with Wast-coat, Breeches, Shoes, Stockins, hat, and all the Accoutrements of an *European*, but all the rest had only Deer-skins about their shoulders, and Seal-skins tied about their middles. They were painted, tho' their natural swarthy colour was easily discern'd; their hair very long, and tied up with a knot behind." Some of them spoke a crude form of English, Archer was pleased to relate, and their manner, if not quite friendly, was at least unthreatening.

He did not think as highly of the next group of natives he encountered. These "were more finely deck'd than the Former, having all of them Copper Pendants in their Ears; but one had a Breastplate of the same Metal a foot long, and half broad; and another had his Head all stuck with Feathers, that rendred him a very frightful Figure. They brought little trifles to Barter, but they were a shy, sly, thievish sort of People."

The encounter was free of incident, however. The sailors happily exchanged the natives' trifles for their own, and the *Concord* sailed on, past more of the craggy coastline in this world so far from home.

Once again, Archer picked up his pen. He noticed "a Lake of fresh Water almost a League in Circuit, and very near the Sea; in the midst of which is another little Island about an Acre in compass, and this [we] thought the most convenient place for the building for a Fort, and therefore began it here. About this Lake there was an infinite number of Tortoises, several sorts of Fowl and Fish too, so that those that liv'd here might have a fair prospect of Provisions enough."

More than the creatures, though, it was the land that impressed Archer: such sweeping vistas, so distant a horizon. Were the fields and hills and valleys as boundless as they seemed? What would it be like to ride the waves of terrain as they had ridden the waves of the

ocean, to measure and map them, to follow them to the horizon—
and perhaps beyond it? What would they find? Archer could see so
much farther here than in the Old World, which, depending on your
frame of mind, was either an intimidating prospect or a bracing one.

When he looked in the other direction, behind him, he saw
even more islands. They popped up from one minute to the next, all
shapes and sizes, scattered in the water and so green in the spring
sunlight that they glowed. One of them we know today as Martha's
Vineyard. Captain Gosnold named another, "a small unpeopled Spot,
and over-run with Trees," in honor of Queen Elizabeth. It

> abounded with Trees of many kinds, which we see here in these
> Parts of the World, so the most remarkable of all were the Sas-
> safras and the Cherry-trees, as they call them. The former are
> well known for their use in Physick,[*] and are no rarities in this
> Island; the latter have this extraordinary in them, that together
> with the Leaf, Bark, and bigness, not different from ours in *Eng-
> land*, the Fruit grows at the end of the Stalk 40 or 50 in a clus-
> ter. The Vines were very numerous here too, and the more
> common Garden and wild Fruits in great abundance.

And there was yet more bounty: "The Minerals were Copper,
Emery-stones, Alabaster, together with some others of a blue Met-
aline colour, which our Author knew not what to make of; some
there were that said 'twas Steel ore, but they ought to have consider'd that tho' Gold Mines are very scarce, yet Steel Mines are certain
much scarcer, and they are never found but where a Brass Mine lies
either at the top or the bottom." Captain Gosnold's crew also found
stones that could be used to build shelters and the walls to surround
them. They would be safe here in addition to being well fed.

They would also be gainfully employed, or at least amused. As
Archer noted, Elizabeth Island "affords also Materials for Dying, and

---

[*]A medicine, most likely a laxative.

for Smoking; and no other yields finer Tobacco than this. The Main Land adjoining, which [we] visited also, was in all respects as charming, as curious Meadows, Groves, Brooks and Rivers cou'd make it."

This was what Gabriel Archer and the others aboard the *Concord* saw when they came to the New World at the dawn of the seventeenth century. But what did they think? What possibilities did they envision, what fancies did they indulge? About these matters Gabriel Archer did not write.

Did he and his fellows believe that in a place so vast, uncharted, and distant from Europe they could one day leave their homeland behind emotionally as well as geographically, that they could lead new and different kinds of lives, lives that would be more enriching for them, truer to their own longings? Did they believe they would be able to make decisions for themselves, worship as they pleased, be governed not by fiat but by their own consent? Did their first look at this part of the earth, where nature ran riot and other humans were few and primitive, make them wonder about erecting a civilization of their own here, something more advanced than what presently existed? Did the expanses of woodlands and bodies of water suggest the opportunity for expansion within the individual? Did the absence of boundaries feel like a release from captivity?

And if some of these musings did enter their minds in the spring of 1602, how far did they go? Could the men from the *Concord* or any of the other ships that landed in America in the earliest days of colonization have foreseen that with religious and political freedom would come another kind of freedom, the freedom to rise from anonymity, to be known and venerated by your fellow citizens without benefit of noble lineage or divine appointment, strictly on the basis of merit? Could they have foreseen that the men who wrote the documents and created the institutions that would ensure those new forms of worship and governance would be rewarded for the rest of time? Books, monuments, paintings, and statues would preserve their images and remind people of their achievements long after the individuals had passed away.

In the century after the *Concord*'s voyage, Benjamin Franklin would become such a celebrity that a modern writer compared his reception in France to that of the Beatles when they first came to the United States. When George Washington retired from the presidency, Americans journeyed to his home at Mount Vernon just as their descendants swooped down on Graceland almost two centuries later, standing at the gates, looking in with hopeful eyes. The same was true for Thomas Jefferson at Monticello, although he would attract a rowdier crowd than Washington, a crowd that sometimes stormed the grounds. So eager was Patrick Henry for a similar kind of notice as a young man that he would resort to chicanery to achieve it and then brag about his misconduct to the very person whom he had most victimized. So desperate for attention as a young man was Alexander Hamilton that he cursed his ambition, finding it an obsession that permitted him, at times, to think of nothing else, to act with no other goal in mind than to advertise himself, to be someone who mattered in the world one day. And, as an old man, John Adams would complain that he had not received enough attention and that too much had been paid to too many others of far more limited accomplishment—and his resentments would inflame him just as ambition had inflamed Hamilton.

These men and the others who became famous in colonial America might never have been famous in an earlier time or in a different place, and perhaps Gabriel Archer and his crewmates felt the first vague stirrings of that knowledge more than a century and a half earlier when they stood on the deck of the *Concord* and looked out, seeing either the end of the world as they had always known it or the unimagined grandeur of a new one.

Part I

The Beginnings of Celebrity

Chapter 1
The Roman Republic

*T*HE MODEL FOR THE COUNTRY that would one day occupy the land Archer had seen, that would one day be known as the United States of America, was the Roman republic, which lasted from 509–27 B.C. The goals of the republic, as expressed by its most respected philosophers and historians, provided the rough draft for notions of equality, justice, and freedom in the British settlements of the New World. And it was the Roman system of government, more than any other document or set of ideals, that became the basis for the new nation. Michael Lind has written that John Adams, Alexander Hamilton, and James Madison, among others, believed the Roman constitution displayed "a stability missing from the faction-ridden city-states of ancient Greece and medieval Italy: a strong chief magistrate and a bicameral legislature with a powerful senate." Adams went further, claiming that "the Roman constitution formed the noblest people, and the greatest power, that has ever existed."

It was not hyperbole, not as far as learned Americans of the eighteenth century were concerned. They not only knew their history but were guided by it. The Founding Fathers succeeded in creating the United States in large part because they were students of the ancient world as much as innovators in their own.

They knew, for instance, that at the head of the Roman republic were two consuls, a check and a balance in its most basic form. Not all the power, however, was theirs. It also resided in two legislative chambers, with the more powerful being the Senate, and in the people — some of the people, at least. No law that the Senate proposed could be enacted until every citizen — that is, every free white male in the republic — had cast his vote. As Lind points out:

> The very name "republic" was a version of the Latin *res publica*. The building that housed the legislature was called the Capitol, not the Parliament; the upper house was the Senate; a creek on Capitol Hill was waggishly named the Tiber, after the river that ran through Rome. The Great Seal of the United States includes two mottoes from Virgil: *Annuit coeptis* (He approves of the beginnings), and *Novus Ordo Seculorum* (a new order of the ages). In the Federalist Papers, Alexander Hamilton, James Madison, and John Jay argued for the ratification of the federal constitution using the name of Publius Valerius Publicola, the first consul of the Roman republic. The enemies of republicanism that they described — faction, avarice, corruption, ambition — were those identified by Cicero, Tacitus, and other Roman writers.

Those enemies and others eventually brought down the republic. Rome gradually reached a point at which it had grown too large and had accumulated too many provinces to be governed from a central seat of power. The result was a regional diffusion of that power, which in turn led to inefficiency, dishonesty, and violence — the end of what seemed to the citizens of a distant future in the New World like a remarkable dream that had for half a millennium come true.

★   ★   ★

The noblest Roman of them all, as far as the Founding Fathers were concerned, was an orator and essayist, a philosopher and a schemer, a public official and public nuisance whom history knows, and knows well, as Cicero. Call him a realistic visionary, a man who knew when to compromise, when to stand firm, and when the best course of action was simply to change the subject. He lived his life as a pragmatist and ended it in a burst of tragic glory.

As a member of the Senate, Cicero led the resistance to the Catiline conspiracy, an attempt by one of Rome's viler denizens to overthrow the republic. Catiline was a known extortionist, the suspected murderer of his stepson, and the seducer of a vestal virgin. When his plans to seize the government were thwarted, his life was spared — perhaps in part because the evidence against him was scant, despite the popular perception of him. But Cicero ordered five of Cataline's fellow conspirators to be executed without benefit of trial, and they were strangled in front of a throng both awestruck and approving. An example had to be made. The sanctity of the republic had to be maintained. Cicero saw that it happened.

Later, after the assassination of Julius Caesar, in which he played no role, Cicero preached to his fellow senators about the perfidy of Caesar's ally, Mark Antony. As a result, Antony soon fled into exile, dismissed to the provinces, and defeated in battle. For a time, Cicero's eminence in the capital was unquestioned.

But politics was an even more treacherous game then than now. Eventually, Cicero's maneuverings landed him on the wrong side of the power structure. He was condemned to death and then killed while trying to escape from his home. "Come here, soldier," he is supposed to have said to Herennius, the leader of the mob that overtook him. "There is nothing proper about what you are doing, but at least make sure you cut off my head *properly*." Moments later, despite what seemed to be sincere misgivings, Herennius slit Cicero's throat.

In the subtitle of the most recent biography of Cicero, Anthony Everitt refers to him as "Rome's greatest politician." For a time he was. At the end of his life, he was not. But he was unarguably the republic's greatest and most enduring man of letters, his writings considered "masterpieces of popularization [which] were one of the most valuable means by which the heritage of classical thought was handed down to posterity." Among his masterpieces were volumes on law, history, culture, political education, and the proper organization of government. In many of them he endorsed the quest for fame.

His full name was Marcus Tullius Cicero, and he was born on January 3, 106 B.C. His father was a scholar — wise, but neither healthy nor wealthy. Of his mother we know little. The orator's name sounds grand to us now, but that is because we know what he became. As Everitt points out, the Latin word *cicero* literally means "chickpea" and was given to the boy, according to several accounts, because an ancestor had a growth at the tip of his nose that looked like a chickpea, perhaps even larger: "When Marcus was about to launch his career as an advocate and politician, friends advised him to change his name to something less ridiculous. 'No,' he replied firmly, 'I am going to make my *cognomen* more famous than those of men like Scaurus and Catalus.' These were two leading Romans of the day, and the point of the remark was that 'Catalus' was the Latin for 'whelp' or 'puppy,' and 'Scaurus' meant 'with large or projecting ankles.' " As things turned out, Cicero was true to his word. The Chickpea became much better known to history than either the Puppy or Large Ankles.

And it was no accident. Cicero worked at renown, desiring "fame and good men's praises," deciding on the best methods of achieving them, and then putting those methods into practice with tireless dedication. For him, this meant a career as an advocate, a lawyer, a more respected position then than it is today. A Roman advocate took an oath to defend his clients only if he believed they were honorable men engaged in honorable pursuits. The clients' ability to pay was not an issue.

Cicero had no reservations about the oath, and his knowledge of the law, combined with his brilliant rhetoric, both improvised and rehearsed, soon made him one of the most highly regarded advocates in the republic. The courtroom, however, was not just the shop in which he worked; it was also the stage on which he performed.

> Despite the fact that the theater was not regarded as a respectable profession, Cicero was fascinated by it and later became a close friend of the best-known actor of his day, Quintus Roscius Gallus. Although he always insisted that oratory and drama were different arts, he modeled his style on Roscius's performances and those of another actor he knew, Clodius Aesopus (who once became so involved in the part he was playing — that of King Agamemnon, overlord of the Greeks — that he ran through and killed a stagehand who happened to cross the stage).

Cicero never got that carried away. Nonetheless, his monologues at trial were gems of theatrical art: superbly delivered, well-reasoned models of clarity and logic that more often than not resulted in victory for his side. He began to build a reputation, but was impatient for it to grow, and, like his fellow stars of the ancient world, was determined that it last the ages. He asked his friend Atticus what history would think of him after a thousand years. Could fame, which sometimes seemed so ephemeral, a quality carried on the faintest of breezes, last a millennium? Atticus could not say.

In search of an answer of his own, Cicero studied his audience. "Once I had realized that the Roman People was rather deaf," he wrote early in his career, "but sharp-eyed, I stopped worrying about what the world *heard* about me. From that day on, I took care to be seen *in person* every day. I lived in the public eye and was always in the Forum. I would not allow my concierge, nor the lateness of the hour, to close the door on any visitor."

By this time, Cicero had grown into a handsome, if not particularly robust, young man, "with full lips, a decisive nose, and beetling brows," features that distinguished him for the rest of his years. He had also grown into a master of self-promotion, studying its fine points as Machiavelli would later study the fine points of political manipulation. Cicero memorized the names of as many well-placed Romans as possible, so that he could greet them as friends — whether he knew them well or not. He also found out where they lived, both their city homes and their country residences, and he would often stroll in front of those structures, hoping to be noticed, always deep in thought (or seeming to be), always the man of sub-stance, his true-to-life role. Sometimes, if the man he hoped to impress was outside, he would greet him warmly, stopping for a few minutes of conversation. He was a glad-hander, a backslapper — but always with a reserve of decorum.

This was not, in his view, mere vanity. "Public esteem is the nurse of the arts," he wrote on one occasion, "and all men are fired to application by fame, whilst those pursuits which meet with gen-eral disapproval always lie neglected."

That he sometimes seemed to care too much about public esteem was obvious to some at the time and to many later. As a young man, he had served the republic admirably as a magistrate in Sicily. But when he returned to Rome, no one congratulated him. No one proposed that a coin bear his profile. Few people even seemed to know where he had been in recent months or what he had done. So indifferent a reception, he admitted, troubled him. Cicero was "intemperately fond of his own glory," wrote the Roman historian Plutarch about this incident a few generations later. "By his insatiable thirst of fame," opined the British poet and dramatist John Dryden in the seventeenth century, "he has lessened his character with succeeding ages."

Cicero received reactions like these in his own day, too. He was rightly accused of braggadocio as much as accomplishment. He also knew that the best way to deal with such charges was to admit them and to confess his self-aggrandizement in a self-deprecating manner. Once, while reviewing his own performance in a public debate, he couldn't help opine that he had done well — yet he did so wryly.

> I brought the house down. And why not, on such a theme — the dignity of our order, concord between Senate and *equites*,[*] uni- son of Italy, remnants of the conspiracy in their death throes, reduced price of grain, internal peace? You should know by now how I can boom away on such topics. I think you must have caught the reverberations in Epirus,[†] and for that reason I won't dwell on the subject.

He further tried to disarm his foes by pointing out the hypocrisy of those philosophers, himself among them, who wrote books in which they criticized the quest for fame and then boldly inscribed their names on the title pages. But lest he go too far down the path of self-effacement, he continued: "The striving for praise is an universal factor in life, and the nobler a man is, the more suscep- tible is he to the sweets of glory."

Yet Cicero was not indiscriminate in his quest for those sweets. He wanted them badly but, in his view, justly, for the right reasons, for what he believed to be the most virtuous of causes. He wanted to be known for his support of the issues he thought important to the success of the Roman republic. He craved admiration for his vision of the republic's future. It is what we would today call enlight- ened self-interest, the realization by a gifted individual that he could satisfy the cultural and political needs of the community at the same time that he satisfied the needs of his own ego. For this reason, the men who created the American republic looked on him as one of their own. Dryden's opinion notwithstanding, Cicero's character didn't suffer in the least.

---

[*]Privileged landowners descended from the ancient Roman calvary.
[†]A nation in the ancient world — in what is now northwest Greece and southern Albania — where Atticus had estates.

Perhaps none of the founders looked up to Cicero more than did John Adams. Certainly none read his works more assiduously. "In all history," Adams declared, "there was no greater statesman and philosopher than Cicero, whose authority should ever carry great weight, and Cicero's decided opinion in favor of the three branches of government was founded on a reason that was timeless, unchangeable." Well before the Revolutionary War, Adams said he was proud that in choosing the law as a profession, he had chosen the same field as Cicero. He was also proud that his friend Jonathan Sewall believed him to be destined for greatness, no matter what his occupation, although he thought Sewall tended to excess when he wrote to Adams that "in future ages, when New England shall have risen to its intended grandeur, it shall be as carefully recorded among the registers of the literati that Adams flourished in the second century after the exode of its first settlers from Great Britain, as it is now that Cicero was born in the six-hundred-and-forty-seventh year after the building of Rome."

And long after the war had ended, Adams was still reading Cicero, some essays for the second and third times — appreciating the stateliness of the prose, reflecting on the precepts of republican government as the Romans had worked them out and the honor that Cicero claimed for his contributions to the cause. Adams believed that these writings prepared him well for the presidency, and after leaving office he quoted Cicero on the conduct of the ideal public official. "Such a man will devote himself entirely to the republic, nor will he covet power or riches. . . . He will adhere closely to justice and equity, that, provided he can preserve these virtues, although he may give offence and create enemies by them, he will set death itself at defiance, rather than abandon his principles." It is how Adams liked to think he had behaved while serving as the nation's second chief executive.

Adams's cousin, the fiery revolutionary and shady journalist Samuel Adams, wrote his calls to arms in the *Boston Gazette* under a variety of pseudonyms. Several of his articles, railing against the presence of British soldiers on the streets of Boston, a presence that eventually led to the Boston Massacre, were signed "Cedant Armae Togae," which means that weapons should yield to togas; i.e., the military should obey civilians. It was one of Cicero's favorite phrases.

Alexander Hamilton, another founder who was at times as much a journalist as a politician and who also took an assumed identity in the press, wrote a series of essays signed "Tully," the English version of Cicero's family name.

John Witherspoon, president of the College of New Jersey, later known as Princeton, called his country home "Tusculum," giving it the same name as Cicero's villa.

Benjamin Franklin cited Cicero as his authority on a variety of matters, such as the importance of virtue to a public man and the duty of a society to care for its less fortunate citizens. In 1744, while still a newspaper man, Franklin reprinted Cicero's essay on aging with a preface he had written himself. A few years later in *Poor Richard's Almanac*, he quoted Cicero's opinion that "There was never any *great* man who was not an *industrious* man."

George Washington probably knew less about Cicero than the other founders, but enough to appreciate the debt that Americans owed him. Hoping to make his stepson a better educated man than he was himself, Washington ordered from an English bookseller Cicero's entire oeuvre, a twenty-volume set, and insisted that the young man memorize its lessons and heed them faithfully. Later, Washington would be called the father of his country, but though the sentiment was true, the wording was not original. The Roman philosopher Cato had given the same title centuries earlier to the man who had thwarted Catiline, among other accomplishments. It was Cicero, not George Washington, whom history first named as *pater patriae*.

John Marshall, who would one day be chief justice of the United States, credited Cicero for most of his own learning. Marshall's college career at William and Mary lasted a mere six weeks, but, having read Cicero, he felt that he was well prepared for a life of public service, once telling his grandsons that the *De Officiis*, Cicero's work about morality, humility, and civic duty, was "among the most valuable treatises in the Latin language, a salutary discourse on the duties and qualities proper to a republican gentleman."

Benjamin Rush, the leading medical man of the revolutionary era as well as one of its most astute social reformers, often cited Cicero in his speeches. Rush was especially fond of insisting that the welfare of the society as a whole was more important than the welfare of any single individual. Cicero had often made the same point. He didn't want to be a god, he didn't want to be a king, he didn't want to become famous by transcending the good of the Roman republic. Rather, his goal was to associate himself with that good and, even more, to be responsible for it as much as possible and receive the congratulations due him for such a commitment.

The same would prove true, many centuries later, of the Americans who formed their own republic.

Chapter 2
The American in Paris

BY 1776, MOST OF BENJAMIN FRANKLIN'S ACCOMPLISHMENTS, as well as his days, were behind him. He had invented the lightning rod, bifocal lenses, America's first copperplate printing press, and a musical instrument called the armonica, for which both Mozart and Beethoven would compose pieces. He had invented a chair that turned into a stepladder, another chair with an arm wide enough to serve as a writing surface, and the stove that bore his name, which, because of its uniquely efficient arrangement of flues, could heat a room twice as effectively using a quarter of the fuel. He had invented a phonetic alphabet, which didn't catch on, and a new kind of street lighting for his fellow colonists, which did. He even invented swim fins, which makes him the only Founding Father to be named to a hall of fame, the International Swimming Hall of Fame. He was as energetically curious a man as America has ever known. "He could not drink a cup of tea without wondering why tea leaves gathered in one configuration rather than another at the bottom," writes Edmund S. Morgan, one of his many biographers.

"He was always devising experiments to help him understand what he saw around him, but he made the whole world his laboratory."

As a journalist, Franklin had learned his trade at his brother's *New England Courant*, going on to own and publish the *Pennsylvania Gazette*, which became one of the colonies' most respected newspapers and one of its most profitable. As an author, he not only had written *Poor Richard's Almanac* (borrowing from many other authors) but had begun work on one of the English language's finest autobiographies, which he never finished. As a scientist, he mapped the flow of the Gulf Stream, conjectured wisely about the earth's magnetic pull, and learned more about electricity than anyone ever had known before. He was chosen for membership in the Royal Society of London, with William Pitt using the occasion to tell the House of Lords that the American's accomplishments ranked him with Sir Isaac Newton. The French respected him no less, naming him a foreign associate of their Royal Academy of Science, an honor as rare as the one the British had bestowed. Frenchmen who experimented with electricity had for some time been known as *franklistes*, a term also favored by those who followed some of Franklin's other scientific pursuits. "He stole the fire of the Heavens," they believed, "and caused the arts to flourish in savage climes."

Franklin had virtually transformed his adopted hometown of Philadelphia, seeing to it that the streets were not only well lighted but paved. He also established the world's first subscription library and public hospital, restructured the police department into a more efficient entity, and organized the first fire department anywhere in North America. He improved mail service between the colonies and founded both the American Philosophical Society and the academy that became the University of Pennsylvania.

Most notably, though, he had been one of the leaders in the movement for independence — submitting the plan that led to the Articles of Confederation and ensuring adequate supplies of paper money so that, after the Revolutionary War began, the Continental Army could be paid from time to time.

Yet in the summer of 1776, that army was not doing well. The war was more than a year old now, and the American forces were in fact fighting with very little force. They were poorly clothed, poorly fed, and in some cases poorly led. They did not have enough weapons or ammunition, and were even shorter on supplies of medicine to treat not only the wounds of battle but the diseases brought on by the horrifyingly unsanitary conditions that accompanied battle. The number of men was also insufficient. Many found a single tour of duty an experience they did not want to repeat, and some even deserted before their tours were over, returning to their shops, farms, and families.

As a result, old man Franklin was asked to come to his country's aid yet again, this time by sailing to Paris to persuade the French to support the colonial cause. It was, many Americans believed, their only chance to succeed. Without outside assistance, they would surely be vanquished, reduced to an even more demeaning status within the British empire than they had known previously. And it was a task that required a special, if not unique, man, someone who combined experience, intelligence, and tact — and all of them in large quantities. Franklin, in the minds of most who knew him, was the only man for the job.

And what a job it was. Despite all that he had achieved in the past, Franklin's mission to France was probably the most important he ever undertook. It was also, as biographer H. W. Brands, recounts, the most difficult.

> For a man of seventy, suffering from gout and assorted lesser afflictions, to leave his home in the middle of a war, to cross a wintry sea patrolled by enemy warships whose commanders could be counted on to know him even if they knew nary another American face, was no small undertaking....Yet Franklin had made his decision that America must be free, and he was determined to pay whatever cost his country required. "I have only a few years to live," he told Benjamin Rush, "and I am resolved to devote them to the work that my fellow citizens

deem proper for me; or speaking as old-clothes dealers do of a remnant of goods, 'You shall have me for what you please.' "

That attitude, wholly sincere, endeared Franklin to his fellow Americans. To the French, however, he proved even more endearing. They greeted him as if he were one of their own, one of their most exceptional own — not just the scientific community that had already honored him, but all Frenchmen, who had heard enough about him to know that he was more than a mere scientist, more than just an inventor, more than a civic planner, reformer, and home-spun philosopher. He was so much more, it seemed, than a single human being, the compiler of the most staggeringly varied list of achievements they had ever known. Before long, Franklin became the first true American celebrity, although it was in Paris rather than in the colonies that he received his first enduring ovations.

The masses took to him quickly. So did the intellectuals, who were growing disenchanted with the monarchy and starting to iden-tify with the masses. Said John Adams, also in France in his nation's service at the time and seldom warmly disposed toward Franklin, "there was scarcely a peasant or citizen, a *valet de chambre*, coachman or footman, a lady's chambermaid or a scullion in a kitchen, who was not familiar with [Franklin], and who did not consider him as a friend of human kind. When they spoke of him, they seemed to think he was to restore the golden age." He was, in other words, the perfect representative of a nascent democracy, toward which the French were moving almost as surely, if not as quickly, as the Amer-icans.

Yet the nobility, who would resist democratic reforms in the bloody revolution of 1789, also found themselves smitten. He was, after all, royalty of a sort himself — although through genius rather than birth. The French royals appreciated the respect with which he treated them, as well as the understanding he showed of the delicacy of his assignment. As Will Durant put it with admirable succinctness,

Franklin "paraded no utopias, talked with reason and good sense, and showed full awareness of the difficulties and the facts. He realized that he was a Protestant, a deist, and a republican seeking help from a Catholic country and a pious king."

It was a French diarist of the time who first recorded the American's appearance in his capital. "The celebrated Franklin arrived at Paris the 21st of December," the man wrote, "and has fixed the eyes of every one upon his slightest proceeding." According to another diarist, "Doctor Franklin arrived a little since from the English colonies, is mightily run after, much feted by the savants."

And he was much studied by all. People bought biographical sketches of Franklin and read as much about him as they could. They bought his collected works, which had appeared in French three years earlier and sold out within a few weeks of his arrival. A volume of Poor Richard's maxims was published not long afterward and went through several printings in the next few years. The French hung portraits of Franklin in their bedrooms and dining rooms and over their hearths. His face appeared on all manner of items, including clocks, rings, busts, medallions, and other pieces of jewelry, vases, snuffboxes, candy boxes, and, according to some reports, the bottoms of chamber pots. You could lift the lid to relieve yourself and smile down at the American master of all trades, who would smile back up. Another version of the chamber pot story comes, with a certain degree of skepticism, from historian David McCullough. "Reputedly," he writes, "the King himself, in a rare show of humor, arranged for [Franklin's likeness] to be hand-painted on the bottom of a Sèvres porcelain chamber pot, as a New Year's day surprise for one of Franklin's adoring ladies at court."

Then again, it might not have been a rare show of humor. It might have been an all-too-frequent display of pique, with Louis XVI becoming envious of the attention the American was attracting and deciding to give Franklin's adoring lady the most jarring of surprises when the time came for her to relieve herself.

Regardless, a multitude of French women adored Franklin — and not just at court. Some of them began to style their hair in a manner reminiscent of the fur cap that Franklin so often wore. Other women expressed their adoration more directly. Knowing of Franklin's reputation with the fairer sex, they tried to form an alliance with him while he was trying to establish one of a different sort with the French government. And the gentlemen didn't seem to mind; Franklin captivated them, too. On one occasion, attending a fashionable Parisian salon, Franklin wore not his usual fur cap but a different chapeau. "Is that white hat a symbol of liberty?" asked his hostess. Franklin's answer is not recorded, but soon a white hat was *de rigueur* for the French male.

Franklin's lack of fashion sense — as perceived by those in Paris who had previously dressed with such elegance in silks and brocades, velvets and laces — became all the rage. Tailors designed deliberately rustic garb to copy the Franklin look and could barely keep up with the demand, so eager were people to attire themselves, as was said at the time, "*à la* Franklin, in coarse cloth . . . and thick shoes," with a waistcoat cut loosely and either a fur cap or a white hat atop the pate. Before long, to dress up was to dress down. The sophisticated Parisians — some of them, at least — were acting like today's upper-class white kids donning the attire of the ghetto: the backward baseball caps and the sagging, oversize pants. Franklin was a delight to them, and they demonstrated it by remaking themselves in his image.

Eventually they demonstrated it in more important ways. After much disappointment, much frustration, and much time, Franklin reached an agreement with the French to send soldiers, rifles, bullets, gunpowder, mortars, and tents to America to aid the rebellion. The French also provided money for the colonists in the form of donations and loans. In other words, France, full-fledged and long established, gave its imprimatur to a band of widely scattered British colonies settled by people fighting for an implausible dream. Due in large part to French assistance, the Americans would win their war for independence — although Franklin, to his everlasting regret, would not be home to see either the turning of the tide on the battlefields or the celebrations afterward. Not until 1785, nine years after first setting foot in France and two years after the war with England had officially ended with the signing of the Treaty of Paris, was he free of diplomatic duties and able to sail back to the country and the people he had represented so well for so long.

The French were sorry, in some cases bereft, to see him go. He had worn his fame as comfortably as his clothes, delighting in the tributes he received and in the expressions of regard that followed him home. The men missed his conviviality, the women his avuncular sex appeal. One woman, a notable Parisienne named Anne-Louise Brillion de Jouy, wrote him shortly after he departed. "Every day I shall remember that a great man, a sage, has wanted to be my friend," she told him. "If it ever pleases you to remember the woman who loved you the most, think of me."

Franklin was not aware of how thoroughly American newspapers had been reporting his diplomatic ventures abroad. He had no idea how he would be received upon his return. As it turned out, his fame was portable, weathering both the years and the ocean transit superbly.

His ship floated into the Market Street wharf in Philadelphia in September 1785, and he heard cannons boom and bells ring in the distance — the unmistakable din of welcome. When it docked, Franklin heard something more subtle, the excited murmur of men and women awaiting him onshore, a solid mass of them not only on the dock but spilling down the side streets that led to it. "We were received by a crowd of people with huzzas and accompanied with acclamations quite to my door," he proudly related — and he was accompanied closely, the crowd pressing in on him as he walked to his residence, wanting a closer look, a touch, a few comments about the voyage or the remarkably productive diplomatic engagements that had preceded it. But when Franklin spoke, few could hear, so loudly were others cheering and singing his praises and bumping into him as they celebrated his homecoming.

Finally, offering a few words to those closest to him, he waved his final good-byes and entered his house, reluctantly closing the door on a throng equally reluctant to disperse. We can imagine him leaning back against the door and sighing in relief, pleased that he had survived the tumultuous journey from the dock — and yet hoping he had still left the metaphorical door open for future plaudits. To John Jay he later wrote: "The affectionate welcome I meet with from my fellow is far beyond my expectations."

Franklin returned to private life with what seemed his old sense of purpose: resuming acquaintances in Philadelphia, picking up correspondence with friends in other colonies and countries, conducting the occasional experiment, reading up on the latest scientific developments abroad, looking in on the police and fire departments to see how they had fared in his absence. But his life did not remain private for long. Two years later his country called on him again, naming him a delegate to the Constitutional Convention, and after that he became president of the Pennsylvania Society for Promoting the Abolition of Slavery. Benjamin Franklin couldn't resist working for causes in which he believed. Nor could he resist the acclaim that greeted such efforts.

A plant had already been named after him, a tree discovered in Georgia in 1765, officially registered as *Franklinia alatamaha*. Perhaps, in years to come, even American women would begin to wear their wigs in a manner suggesting a fur cap.

Franklin's regard for fame wavered — though not much and not often. In 1779, he hinted at misgivings in a letter to his daughter, commenting on all the items for sale in Paris that bore his likeness: "These, with the pictures, busts and prints (of which copies upon copies are spread everywhere), have made your father's face as well known as that of the moon, so that he durst not do anything that would oblige him to run away, as his phiz* would discover him wherever he should venture to show it."

Some years earlier, in *Poor Richard's Almanac*, Franklin had written more skeptically of fame, especially the lasting kind, which he apparently did not think possible.

> And with what rare *Inventions* do we strive
>   *Ourselves* then to survive.
> Some with vast costly *Tombs* would purchase it,
>   And by the *Proofs of Death* pretend to *live.*
> *Here lies the Great* — False Marble, where?
>   Nothing but *small* and *sordid* Dust lies there.

But the poem and the letter to his daughter were exceptions, Franklin giving in to a mood rather than examining his views at a deeper level. More often than not, he welcomed public attention as he welcomed a glass of Madeira after a good meal. He had set out in life to "imitate Jesus and Socrates," he admitted as a young man, and they were two of the most famous people who ever lived. Writing as Poor Richard, a year before the preceding verse, he confessed his longing to be known but this time rued the odds against it:

> The Hope of acquiring lasting FAME is, with many Authors, a most powerful Motive to Writing. Some, tho' few, have succeeded; and others, tho' perhaps fewer, may succeed hereafter, and be as well known to Posterity by their Works, as the Antients are to us. We Philomaths, as ambitious of Fame as any other Writers whatever, after all our painful Watching and laborious Calculations, have the constant Mortification to see our Works thrown by at the End of the Year, and treated as mere Waste Paper. Our only Consolation is, that short-lived as they are, they out live those of most of our Contemporaries.

---

*Face, shortened from physiognomy.

At least one of Franklin's friends, Nathaniel Evans, did not think Franklin's works would be short-lived, even before those works included his diplomatic mission to France, and on a surprising occasion, he wrote to Franklin and told him so in a poem:

> Long had we, lost in grateful wonder, view'd
> Each gen'rous act the patriot soul pursu'd;
> Our little State resounds thy just applause,
> And pleas'd from thee new fame and honour draws.

And on the paean went, this verse from an Anglican clergyman who had known Franklin a long time and declared that those who had denigrated him in the past must now concede his sanctified state, must admit that he had proven himself a man of "superior worth," that he possessed "true eminence of mind," that all who knew of his deeds and had judged them objectively had in fact long been "fixt with rapture." On and on Evans went like this, the inspiration for his encomiums being nothing more than having heard Franklin play a few tunes on his armonica! Or were they, as Evans insisted on calling them, not really tunes at all but, as rendered by the instrument's inventor, "lambent lightnings"?

Franklin might have appreciated the poem, but certainly not the reason for it. Jesus and Socrates had earned their places in history for reasons far more profound than musical tinkering. They had lived the kinds of lives that enlightened the world both spiritually and intellectually, through the words they spoke, the acts they performed, and the examples they set. Franklin believed that he, too, was living that kind of life, if not to the same extent as his idols. He had served his city through the improvements he devised and implemented, and would serve his country both at home and abroad. It seemed only natural, then, that he receive the gratitude of those who were his beneficiaries — a kind word when the time was right — and enough of a foothold in their memories to ensure that the right times would be many.

He didn't demand public notice, and certainly didn't plead for it, but his feelings were clear and always had been. Many years before his stay in Paris, even before his transformation of Philadelphia was complete, he had received a letter from the physician Jared Eliot, a more discriminating friend than Evans. Eliot told Franklin that "the Love of Praise" was common in human beings, and nothing of which the Almighty would disapprove. Franklin could not have agreed more heartily; "it *reigns more or less in every Heart*," he told Eliot, "tho' we are generally Hypocrites, in that respect, and pretend to disregard Praise, and that our nice modest Ears are offended, forsooth, with what one of the Antients calls *the Sweetest kind of Music*."

Sweeter, certainly, than anything that could be played on the armonica.

In writing of the founders and their attitude toward renown, historian Douglass Adair has referred to "egotism transmuted gloriously into public service." Had Franklin heard the phrase applied to him, not only would he have agreed, he would have chuckled at its aptness and perhaps even purloined it for *Poor Richard's Almanac*.

Chapter 3
Americans at Home

*H*AVING SIGNED THE DECLARATION OF INDEPENDENCE, James Wilson is regarded as one of the Founding Fathers. Having had several of his ideas incorporated into the Constitution, he was respected by the delegates to the Constitutional Convention and viewed favorably by those who supported the document. Others looked on him favorably for different reasons. Though slower than some of his countrymen to declare his support for freedom from the British, he eventually changed his mind and became one of the colonies' most astute analysts of Parliament. People turned to him for explanations of seemingly inexplicable edicts such as the Stamp Act, the Townshend Acts, and the Intolerable Acts. Later he raised his voice, loudly and often, for the abolition of slavery, declaring himself certain it would happen, but not soon. "The period is more distant than I could wish," he admitted sadly. And when the College of Philadelphia began to offer courses in the law, Wilson became its first professor.

But few know his name today. Even to those who study the

colonial era and write about it, he is more likely to show up in a footnote or a list than as the subject of his own chapter or even paragraph. Yet it was James Wilson, more than anyone else, who served as the spokesman for renown in late eighteenth-century America, studying its means, its ends, its byproducts — and endorsing it with an almost religious fervor. He was, in fact, the first American to preach the gospel of acclaim, and his sermons, issued from law-school lecterns rather than pulpits, were plentiful.

"The love of honest and well earned fame is rooted in honest and susceptible minds," Wilson said. "Can there be a stronger incentive to the operations of this passion, than the hope of becoming the object of well founded and distinguishing applause? Can there be a more complete gratification of this passion, than the satisfaction of knowing that this applause is given — that it is given upon the most honourable principles, and acquired by the most honourable pursuits?"

That was the key, Wilson believed — honorable pursuits: "The wisest and most benign constitution of a rational and moral system is that . . . in which the degree of social affection, most useful to the system, is, at the same time, productive of the greatest happiness to the individual." Conversely, Wilson stated that the person "who acts on such principles, and is governed by such affections, as sever him from the common good and publick interest, works, in reality, towards his own misery."

Wilson raised these topics on numerous occasions with his law students, encouraging them to seek the rewards that would be theirs if they mastered their material and conducted their practices with integrity. "The love of reputation and the fear of dishonour are, by the all-gracious Author of our existence, implanted in our breasts, for purposes the most beneficent and wise. Let not these principles be deemed the growth of dispositions only which are weak or vain; they flourish most luxuriantly in minds, the strongest and, let me add, the most humble." And, most directly, if a little repetitiously, Wilson raised the following question: "I will not appeal to vanity, and ask, if any thing can be more flattering, than to *obtain* the praises and acclamations of others. But I will appeal to conscious rectitude, and ask, whether any thing can be more satisfactory, than to *deserve* the regard and esteem."

Wilson's notion of fame is the same as Cicero's, and the latter inspired Wilson to serve as fame's promoter. As he explained on one occasion to a friend, "What . . . can be intrinsically more dignified than to assist in forming a future Cicero or [Sir Francis] Bacon?"

Unfortunately for Wilson, he did not form himself into a Cicero. He was *too* slow to favor independence, some thought, and they never quite forgave him. He earned more enmity later by opposing some of the provisions of Pennsylvania's constitution, although his objections were overridden and the document was approved in 1776. He also fought against price controls, which many believed were necessary to cope with the inflation brought on by the Revolutionary War.

His contributions to the federal constitution had won him praise, but not as much as he thought he deserved. He expected President Washington to reward him by naming him the first chief justice of the United States. Instead, Washington appointed him to the Supreme Court, but as an associate justice under John Jay. Wilson was disappointed, and in turn disappointed Washington and his fellow members of the bench. When cases came before the Court, Wilson often seemed inattentive, writing few opinions and, when he did, offering banalities more than insights. Neither his attendance nor his attitude won him admirers.

Worse, Wilson was accused of trying to influence legislation that would have been favorable to land speculators, then becoming one himself, investing in large tracts of property in at least three colonies and losing large sums of money in each. Soon there was a movement under way to impeach him, and with that he had achieved another first: no American before Wilson had ever faced such a threat.

Initially he couldn't believe it. He thought he had done nothing wrong in his deals and made his opinion unequivocally known. Then he panicked, trying to recoup his losses with a complicated scheme to extract money from newly arrived European settlers. This last venture was not only as unsuccessful as his previous ones, but it was illegal: a patent scam. A warrant was issued for Wilson's arrest, and rather than face it, he ran, fleeing from Philadelphia to Burlington, New Jersey, where he hid with a friend, an act of desperation that made him — yet another distinction — the only person in the history of the United States ever to hold the positions of member of the Supreme Court and fugitive from the law at the same time.

He was not a fugitive for long, however. Authorities in Burlington arrested him and kept him in jail until his son "managed to squeeze from stones enough money to provide bail." His son wanted to take him home to face the charges against him. Instead, Wilson fled again, and after being "hunted like a wild beast," as he complained, he ended up at the home of a fellow jurist in North Carolina, appearing at the man's house in a highly agitated state, cursing the events that had driven him into exile and unable to calm himself, despite his friend's best efforts to provide solace. His friend told Wilson he could stay as long as he wanted, and at this Wilson finally seemed relieved.

But a few days after arriving, Wilson came down with malaria. Two or three weeks later he suffered a stroke, and the next month he died, never having cleared his name, never having achieved anything beyond mediocrity as a jurist before becoming a criminal. Wilson was fifty-eight years old.

He had hoped to be famous, but his anonymity turned out to be a gift, history's way of shielding a man who had strayed so far after commending so passionately his era's regard for renown.

Here are some snapshots of fame, taken at either end of a period of more than a decade, from the album of the man who appointed Wilson to the Supreme Court, an album that bulges with scenes of approbation and gratitude:

1775: The Revolutionary War had barely begun. Americans had lost the battle of Bunker Hill, and George Washington had not yet assumed formal command of the Continental Army. Yet his countrymen were already counting on him, expecting the best, and in a few extraordinary cases demonstrating their confidence in his eventual success by naming their children after him, which they did for years to come. Whenever he could, he expressed his appreciation. "In offering my respects to Mrs. Reed," Washington wrote to his adjutant general Joseph Reed a few years later, with battles raging all around him and far better uses for his time than writing thank-you notes, "I must be permitted to accompany them with a tender of my very warm acknowledgments to her and you for the civilities and attention both of you have been pleased to show Mrs. Washington; and for the honor you have done me in calling the young Christian by my name."

Also in 1775: Shortly after taking his place at the head of American troops, Washington received letters of congratulation from the legislatures of New York and Massachusetts. They were addressed to "His Excellency, George Washington." Biographer Joseph J. Ellis writes: "To be sure, 'His Excellency' is not quite the same thing as 'His Majesty,' but throughout the summer and fall of 1775, even as delegates to the Continental Congress struggled to sustain the fiction that George III remained a friend to American liberty, poets and balladeers were already replacing the British George with an American version of the same name."

1776: Not satisfied with naming their children after Washington, Americans started naming places in his honor. The first seems to have been Stoughtonham Township in Massachusetts — and this at a time when the war was going poorly and the general's name wouldn't necessarily have made the township proud. When the tide finally turned in favor of the colonists, the pace of the naming picked up. Soon most colonies had a town or village called Washington.

Also in 1776: The remarkable Phillis Wheatley, a slave and a poet, wrote an ode to Washington:

Thee, first in peace and honours, — we demand
The grace and glory of thy martial band.
Fam'd for thy valour, for thy virtues more,
Hear every tongue thy guardian and implore! . . .
Proceed, great chief, with virtue on thy side,
Thy ev'ry action let the goddess guide.
A crown, a mansion, and a throne that shine,
With gold unfading, *Washington!* Be thine.

1789: As Washington proceeded from Mount Vernon to New York to be sworn in as America's first president, he was greeted in unprecedented fashion with "an almost uninterrupted series of banquets, speeches, toasts, parades, and all the other ceremonies that a small country could devise." Continues biographer Richard Brookhiser, "In Philadelphia, twenty thousand people turned out to cheer him along; the population of the city was twenty-eight thousand." In Trenton, a chorus of girls sang to him:

Virgins fair and matrons grave,
Those thy conquering arms did save,
Build for thee triumphant bowers.
Strew, ye fair, his way with flowers —
Strew your hero's way with flowers.

And they did just that: the young ladies carried baskets of freshly picked petals and scattered them on the ground before Washington's procession.

And from the *Gazette of the United States*, a rabidly pro-Washington newspaper, as inauguration day grew closer:

Far be the din of arms,
Henceforth the olive's charms
Shall war preclude:

These shores a HEAD shall own,
Unsully'd be a throne,
Our much lov'd WASHINGTON,
    The great, the good.

Washington was always sensitive of the effect he had on those around him, "constantly testing public opinion and tailoring his actions to suit it," his military actions as well as his later political actions. But it is more accurate to say that fame came to him as a consequence of his persona and abilities than that he avidly sought it, and, unlike Franklin, he wasn't at ease when it arrived. In fact, he seldom made direct references to fame, perhaps not wanting to admit it was on his mind. In his speech and writings, he was much more likely to refer to his reputation, which is to say that he thought in terms of quantity rather than quality. Fame means that people know your name, reputation that they know your deeds and have judged them; the latter number will inevitably be smaller than the former. And the latter was of more concern to Washington than the former, even if it was under challenge. "Whensoever I shall be convinced," he told his friend Henry Lee, "that the good of my country requires my reputation to put at risk, regard for my own fame will not come in competition with an object of so much magnitude."

Washington cared as well for the reputation of his men. Once, when Rudolphus Ritzema, one of his soldiers, was charged with misconduct, Washington summoned him and asked for an explanation. Ritzema swore that he had been falsely accused, that he had never behaved improperly either in uniform or out. Nonetheless, he told Washington he thought it best for the sake of the troops' morale that he resign his commission.

Washington disagreed. He urged Ritzema to stay, to fight his accusers no less than he had been fighting the British: "the Malice of your worst Enemies cannot do the least injury to your Reputation, which to a Soldier ought ever to be dearer than life."

The first major engagement of the Revolutionary War that Washington commanded was the battle of Brandywine in Pennsylvania in September 1777. He lost. His troops retreated, and the British occupied Philadelphia. It was as much a personal embarrassment to the colonists as a strategic one. Less than a month later, Washington led his men into the battle of Germantown, also in Pennsylvania, where the British again proved victorious. Ritzema was at his side, reputation restored. Washington's, however, which had gotten off to a dubious start, was still not improving.

It was for this reason, at least in part, that he did not want his reputation to depend solely on results. He also wanted to be judged on his character. Results, especially in battle, were subject to all manner of variables: unexpected weather, unknown terrain, vagaries of supply, the health and psychological well-being of the troops, unforeseen maneuvers by the enemy, insufficiently supportive colonial legislatures. These were factors a man could not control. What he could control was his reaction to the variables. Character was a constant.

When he accepted the leadership of the Continental Army, Washington had written to his wife that the position filled him with "inexpressible concern." Still, "it was utterly out of my power to refuse this appointment without exposing my character to such censures, as would have reflected dishonour upon myself, and given pain to my friends — this I am sure could not, and ought not to be pleasing to you, & must have lessend me considerably in my own esteem."

By the time the war was over, of course, Washington's reputation had long since recovered from Brandywine and Germantown, and his character was so well respected by all who knew him that the two qualities had become something of a national monument. After one of his victorious battles, he was pleased "to hear from different Quarters, that my reputation stands fair, that my conduct hitherto has given universal satisfaction."

It stood especially fair to the men who served under him. They knew what kind of man Washington was under both physical and emotional duress, and, when he called them together in New York in December 1783 to say good-bye, the Continental Army now disbanded and the quest for nationhood beginning, words did not come easily.

> Washington said, "I cannot come to each of you, but shall feel obliged if each of you will come and take me by the hand." General Knox was nearest. He "turned to the Commander in Chief, who suffused in tears, was incapable of utterance, but grasped his hand; when they embraced each other in silence. In the same affectionate manner," so continued the reminiscences of Major Benjamin Tallmadge, "every officer in the room marched up to, kissed, and parted with his general in chief. Such a scene of sorrow and weeping I had never before witnessed. . . . The *simple thought* . . . that we should see his face no more in this world seemed to me utterly insupportable."

Washington left the room moments later, having said nothing else, obviously shaken, perhaps more moved than he had ever been before. Yet despite the American triumph, he remained apprehensive about his reputation — no longer fearing it was insufficient but, to the contrary, that it had been bloated beyond the extent to which he could live up to it. He was now left vulnerable, exposed. He knew that public adulation and public scorn were closer than they seemed, kin more than opposites. Until the night of the teary farewells, he had maintained a certain aloofness to his fellow soldiers. Some years earlier, advising one of his men how best to lead his fellows in battle, Washington gave the following advice: "Be easy and condescending* in your deportment to your officers, but not too familiar," he is quoted as saying, "lest you subject yourself to a want of that respect, which is necessary to support a proper command."

---

*The word had a different connotation then than it does today, meaning being kind to inferiors or subordinates.

It was a difficult feat, keeping to yourself while maintaining the right amount of proximity to others. Abigail Adams thought she knew how Washington managed it. The wife of John and mother of John Quincy — who named his own son George Washington Adams — she wrote a letter to her husband in 1790 in which she offered her analysis. Washington, she said, "is polite with dignity, affable without familiarity, distant without Haughtyness, Grave without Austerity, Modest, wise and Good."

And his reputation swelled even more when he appeared to turn his back on the fame that the Revolutionary War had brought him. Who had ever heard of such a thing? Would Cicero have done it? Yet after the war, Washington did not seek to become dictator of the victorious colonies as some of his enemies had feared. Instead, he retired to his Mount Vernon home and for a time showed little interest in matters of government or diplomacy, much less a desire to influence them. Breeding mules occupied him now; he experimented with crop rotation; he tried to raise money to build canals along the Potomac and the James rivers, which he believed would encourage trade and thus increase commerce among the states. Said his aide David Humphreys, who accompanied Washington on the journey from battlefield honor to Mount Vernon, "No person who had not the advantage of being present when General Washington received the intelligence of the peace, and who did not accompany him to his domestic retirement, can describe the relief which that joyful event brought to his laboring mind, or the satisfaction with which he withdrew to the shades of private life."

Even George III, the king of England whose army Washington had dispatched and whose vision of empire he had so dramatically shrunk, was impressed, concluding that by giving up power voluntarily, Washington had proven himself "the greatest man in the world." Yet when Benjamin Franklin sailed back to Philadelphia in 1785 after his triumphant years in France, Washington was a mere farmer and trader and claimed, at least for the foreseeable future, to want nothing more.

*   *   *

Franklin and Washington were among the oldest of the Founding Fathers, with the former outdistancing the latter by twenty-six years. Patrick Henry was four years older than Washington and by 1785 had already uttered most of the fiery rhetoric for which history remembers him. Sam Adams, ten years older than Washington, was perhaps the most fervent of patriots, a man whose rabble-rousing and often fictitious journalism had done as much to bring about the war as any legislative decision made by any colonial assembly. His articles in the *Boston Gazette* on behalf of an independent America were the printed counterpart to Henry's impassioned speeches.

Yet Adams was less concerned with perpetuating his name than any of the other founders. "Seeking fame as little as fortune," wrote a man who knew him well, "and office less than either, he aimed steadily at the good of his country and the best interests of mankind." Adams himself would go no further than to say that "the Man who nobly vindicates the Rights of his Country & Mankind shall stand foremost in the List of fame," and although he surely thought such a description applied to him, he was not the sort to make such a claim publicly.

The other founders were still working on their fame in 1785.

Thomas Jefferson, already known as the principal author of the Declaration of Independence and universally applauded for the eloquence of his sentiments, had since seen his luster dim. In 1779 the Virginia legislature elected him governor, and the timing couldn't have been worse. The country was at war, and the colony, although not the site of any major battles during Jefferson's tenure, was host to a number of skirmishes, in which homes were destroyed, fields were trampled, crops were torched, animals were slaughtered, and militiamen were slain. Virginia's economy suffered under Jefferson, more than that of any other colony during the war, and he suffered an even greater loss of prestige when he fled from British troops descending on his home at Monticello. Jefferson thought he had no choice but to flee. Others accused him of cowardice in the face of adversity.

Jefferson further alienated Virginians by refusing to continue as governor, departing from office before finishing his second term and forcing the legislature to choose his successor. He believed, he said, that in a time of war the position should be held by a man with military experience, and Jefferson, as his constituents well knew, had none. By stepping down, he claimed to be acting in the colony's best interests. But by stepping down so precipitously, he left the office vacant, and inefficiency and disorder prevailed in the statehouse when neither could be afforded.

Nonetheless, Jefferson regained enough of his good name to be elected to Congress in the war's final year, and the year after that he joined Franklin and John Adams as ministers in France. Jefferson later became the nation's first secretary of state under Washington, its second vice president under Adams, and its third president, elected for two terms and serving them in full. Jefferson held more high government offices than any of the other founders and was the most famous of the group not to know what to make of his fame. It is no surprise. He was also the most brilliant man of his era to spend so much time confused about so many other things.

In the fall of 1786, a widower now for four years, Jefferson fell in love with a married woman named Maria Cosway, "a golden-haired, languishing Anglo-Italian, graceful to affectation, and highly accomplished, especially in music." They met in France, and for the next month and a half the two of them were together almost daily, taking in all the sights of Paris, enjoying each other more than the parks and edifices, statues and paintings. They read to each other from their favorite books, dined together in quiet corners, rode in carriages from place to place, holding hands and whispering over the clatter of the wheels. Maria's husband, the miniaturist Richard Cosway, was hard at work on commissions at the time and seemed pleased that his wife had found so notable a man as Jefferson to serve as her escort.

But the relationship was not to last, and both Jefferson and Maria knew it wouldn't from the start. She was reluctant to leave her husband, while Jefferson still mourned for his late wife, unable to commit to someone else and guilty about courting a married woman. Yet Jefferson wanted to make a commitment, at least at times, and Maria wanted him to make that commitment to her, at least at times. They were as halting and uncertain in their feelings toward each other as a pair of teenagers.

Nowhere was this hesitation more evident than in a letter Jefferson wrote to Maria on October 12, 1786, shortly after the Cosways left Paris, a parting that both Jefferson and Maria feared might be permanent. The letter was an imaginary dialogue between the author's head and heart, and is one of the most famous pieces of correspondence in the Jefferson archives.

HEAD. . . . You confess your follies indeed; but still you hug & cherish them; & no reformation can be hoped, where there is no repentance.

HEART. Oh, my friend! This is no moment to upbraid my foibles. I am rent into fragments by the force of my grief! If you have any balm, pour it into my wounds; if none, do not harrow them by new torments.

And later:

HEAD. . . . see what you suffer: & [the Cosways'] return too depends on too many circumstances that if you had a grain of prudence you would not count upon it. Upon the whole it is improbable & therefore you should abandon the idea of ever seeing them again.

HEART. May heaven abandon me if I do!

HEAD. Very well. Suppose then they come back. They are to stay two months, & when these are expired what is to follow? Perhaps you flatter yourself they may come to America?

HEART. God only knows what is to happen. I see nothing impossible in that supposition. And I see things wonderfully contrived sometimes to make us happy.

And finally, a show of pessimism, or at least caution, which may have been at the core of much of Jefferson's fretfulness about his relationship with Maria Cosway.

HEAD. . . . To avoid those eternal distresses, to which you are forever exposing us, you must learn to look forward before you take a step which may interest our peace.

The heart gets much more space in the letter than does its counterpart. But it is statements like the preceding that seem to give the ultimate victory to the head.

The letter is typical of Jefferson, not just because of the occasional sophomoric cast to his erudition, but because of that curious ability of his to see both sides of an issue yet to stand paralyzed by his breadth of vision rather than inspired to a solution.

This was the case not just in matters of romance. Jefferson was, after all, a man who disdained slavery in his writings and public pronouncements, yet supported it through his ownership of blacks at Monticello. He was a man who especially scorned miscegenation, detesting his father-in-law's relationship with the slave Betty Hemings, yet according to modern DNA testing, Jefferson committed it himself with Betty's daughter, his own slave Sally. He was a man with no patience for the teachings of the Anglican church and was never able to escape charges of atheism, yet he called several clergymen friends, drafted his own version of the New Testament, and supported religion through his authorship of the Statute of Virginia for Religious Freedom, which he later referred to as one of the proudest accomplishments of his life. He thought that if a government borrowed money, in time it would cease to function, yet he spent virtually his entire adult life in debt. He believed in a broad education with diverse points of view, yet would not hire professors for the law school at his University of Virginia unless he agreed with their positions on virtually all matters, nor would he allow books into the law school library unless they passed the same test. He railed at the notion of big government, fighting for years against the Hamiltonian concept of federalism, insisting "that government is best which governs least," yet as president he created the biggest government yet, one that sometimes, as in the case of the Louisiana Purchase, ignored the will of the House and Senate altogether. "The less we say about the constitutional difficulties respecting Louisiana," he confided to James Madison, his secretary of state, as he prepared to make the deal, "the better."

It's no wonder, then, that Jefferson was of two minds about fame. That he wanted it for himself, on occasion and on his own terms, is undeniable. He was proud of drafting the Declaration of Independence and pleased that so many people credited him. No less did he shrink from public notice for his accomplishments as secretary of state and president, as the founder of the University of Virginia and the architect of Monticello.

But just as praise heartened him, disapproval laid him low. In his second presidential term, Jefferson demanded an embargo of all British goods into America for a time, and the measure proved to be, in the opinion of historian Kenneth Davis, "one of the most unpopular and unsuccessful acts in American history." Jefferson was inconsolable, certain that future generations would think ill of him if they thought anything at all. In an 1858 biography by Samuel Schmucker, Jefferson is described as a man with "a pusillanimous and morbid terror of popular censure, and an insatiable thirsting after popular praise."

But he could be cutting in his assessment of others who also thirsted for praise. When Patrick Henry's first biographer, William Wirt, asked for Jefferson's assessment of his subject, Jefferson replied that Henry's character was "of mixed aspect. . . . He had a consummate knowledge of the human heart, which directing the efforts of his eloquence enabled him to attain a degree of popularity with the people at large never perhaps equaled." But, Jefferson said, Henry was also "avaritious & rotten hearted. His two great passions were the love of money & of fame: but when these came into competition the former predominated."

Like Washington, Jefferson spent little time addressing fame in his correspondence. But when he did, the contradictions were apparent and usually unresolved. Let us cast them as he might have done.

HEAD. In a letter to his friend Peter Carr the year before he met Maria Cosway, Jefferson encouraged him "to pursue the interests of your country, the interests of your friends, and your own interests also, with the purest integrity, the most chaste honor. The defect of these virtues can never be made up by all the other acquirements of body and mind. Make these then your first object. Give up money, give up fame."

HEART. In the same letter, he wished Carr "fame and promotion in your own country."

HEAD. Many years later, writing to John Adams, Jefferson disparaged the notion of "present fame," or at least warned against behaving improperly to achieve it. Fame simply wasn't worth the price you had to pay.

HEART. A few paragraphs later, Jefferson speaks of an earlier time, of calculations "which would have been deemed honorable . . . of a regard for honest fame and the esteem of our fellow men."

HEAD. Of the Marquis de Lafayette, French hero of the American Revolution, Jefferson was less enamored than many of his countrymen: "His foible is a canine appetite for popularity and fame."

HEART. But with popularity and fame would come reputation, perhaps the kind of reputation Washington so valued, "and a reputation once established will maintain itself for ages."

For Jefferson, this most indecisive of the great colonial decision makers, fame was yet one more issue on which he couldn't take a stand.

★   ★   ★

As a young man, not quite twenty-one years old, John Adams did take a stand: he wanted to be a lawyer. But when he announced this desire to his parents, they were less than enthusiastic.

> They replied that the Town of Boston was full of Lawyers and many of them established Characters for long Experience, great Abilities and extensive Fame, who might be jealous of such a Novelty as a Lawyer in the Country part of their County, and might be induced to obstruct me. I returned that I was not wholly unknown to some of the most celebrated of those Gentlemen, that I believed they had too much candour and Generosity to injure a young Man, and at all Events I could but try the experiment, and if I should find no hope of Success I should then think of some other place or some other course.

Perhaps, Adams might have thought, Cicero had similar feelings when starting out. Adams often read aloud to himself from a copy of Cicero's *Orations* — sometimes for consolation, sometimes for edification. To do so, he explained, "exercises my lungs, raises my spirits, opens my pores, quickens the circulation, and so contributes much to health."

But there were reasons to take up the legal trade other than following in Cicero's footsteps. The profession had been highly regarded in Western culture even before the rise of Rome, and most of the leading figures of colonial America had studied law at one point or another. Adams wanted to join their company. "It will be hard work," he wrote to a friend, "but the more difficult and dangerous the enterprise, a higher crown of laurel is bestowed on the conqueror."

It was hard work indeed. Adams sweated at his chosen field no less than a blacksmith at his forge. He moved in with a lawyer named James Putnam and, as he continued to earn a meager living by teaching during the day, read the law under Putnam's tutelage at night. He studied hour after hour, week after week, season after season. One of the books he had to master was *Pleas of the Crown* by William

Hawkins, which weighed eight pounds. He also slogged his way through multivolume works by such esteemed figures as Edward Coke and William Blackstone; these weighed less but were no more riveting. He read statute books by the score, learning what was allowed in Massachusetts and what was not, and deciding what should and should not be allowed in the future and why. It was, he said, the driest subject matter he had ever encountered.

And so there were nights when his mind would wander, when he would look out the window of Putnam's room at a starless sky and wish he were doing something else, anything else — or nothing at all. He wished his books either weighed less or were more interesting. At the very least, he wished it were morning. As biographer James Grant relates, he decided to make another stand: "In exchange for the hours spent in captivity, there must be fame, fortune, or something." Adams sought his reward as diligently as he sought his vocation. Had he known of the young man's resolve, the not-yet-disgraced James Wilson would have been proud.

Adams had been practicing law for less than a year when he picked up his pen, opened his diary, and subjected himself to a thorough cross-examination.

> Reputation ought to be the perpetual object of my Thoughts, and Aim of my Behaviour. How shall I gain a Reputation! How shall I Spread an Opinion of myself as a lawyer of distinguished Genius, Learning, and Virtue. Shall I make frequent Visits in the Neighbourhood and converse familiarly with Men, Women and Children in their own Style, on the common Tittletattle of the Town, and the ordinary Concerns of a family, and so take every fair opportunity of shewing my Knowledge in the Law? But this will require much Thought, and Time, and a very particular Knowledge of the Province Law, and common Matters, of which I know much less than I do of the Roman Law. This would take up too Much Thought and Time and Province Law.

Not long afterward, Adams concluded that he would need the assistance of events if he were to make a name for himself. "In short," he wrote, "I never shall shine, till some animating Occasion calls forth all my Powers." Of course, some of the most animating occasions in American history were only a few years away.

Later still, considering the prospects of men and women from the Old World who had not yet settled in the colonies but would one day make the voyage, he hoped they would find the newer shore an "Asylum of all the discontented, turbulent, profligate and Desperate from all Parts of Europe," and that once arrived here these people would know "fame, Popularity, Station and Power."

Yet like Jefferson, Adams, too, was ambivalent. Tellingly, he did not bother to capitalize "fame" in the preceding list. And no less tellingly, he wrote, "No man is entirely free from weakness and imperfection in this life. Men of the most exalted Genius and active minds are generally perfect slaves to the love of Fame. They sometimes descend to as mean tricks and artifices, in pursuit of Honour or Reputation, as the Miser descends to, in pursuit of Gold." That pursuit, Adams believed, more often than not left a man unfulfilled, because he "is miserable every moment when he does not snuff the incense."

But Jefferson seemed genuinely indecisive about fame's merits, his skepticism intellectual more than emotional. Adams, on the other hand, although he shared some of those misgivings, was dubious about acclaim because he feared he would never achieve it, at least not to the extent he desired, and he denigrated the condition to cushion his fall. Adams didn't lack confidence in his merits so much as he did in the ability or willingness of others to recognize and applaud them. He knew he didn't make the same striking impression that Washington did, didn't elicit so animated a response with his oratory as Henry, didn't impress with his quiet intelligence like Jefferson. He was the least charismatic of the Founding Fathers and often the least pleasant. A short, squat man who sometimes talked too much and too earnestly, who held a grudge too long and expressed it too fiercely, he had more of the pedagogue in him than the celebrity and possibly even less fashion sense than Franklin. He suspected people would not look deeply enough to see that he was, in most substantive ways, the equal of these men.

And so he sometimes turned on fame with a vengeance. He didn't want the "Noisy applause, and servile Homage" of the masses, he wrote to a friend early in his lawyering days. "And Reason will despize equally, a blind undistinguishing Adoration of what the World calls fame. She is neither a Goddess to be loved, nor a Demon to be feared, but an unsubstantial Phantom existing only in Imagination."

In fact, Adams could have written his own head-and-heart dialogue on the subject of celebrity. But he eventually attracted all the notice he could have imagined in those early days of struggle at the law books, and would invariably be moved by the ways in which it was displayed, his hard edges softening at times more than his acquaintances thought possible. As early as 1770, still just a Massachusetts lawyer, he wrote the following in his diary:

> I have received such Blessings and enjoyed such Tears of Transport — and there is no greater Pleasure, or Consolation! Journeying to Plymouth, I found a Man, who either knew me before, or by enquiring of some Person then present, discovered who I was. He went out and saddled my Horse and bridled him, and held the Stirrup while I mounted. Mr. Adams, says he, as a Man of Liberty, I respect you. God bless you! I'le stand by you, while I live, and from hence to Cape Cod you wont find 10 Men amiss.

Adams rode off glowing.

Yet several years later, after meeting many more men willing to stand by him, he was more restrained in his reaction: "I cannot say that my desire of Fame increases. It has been Strong in some Parts of my Life but never so strong as my Love of honesty. I never in my Life that I know of sacrificed my Principles or Duty to Popularity, or

Reputation. I hope I am now too old ever to do it. But one knows not how trials may be borne, till they are made."

His desire for fame might not have increased, but, as he held ever higher offices in his new nation's government, he could not help but become more and more noticed, more and more the subject of conversation. As vice president, he became the subject of verse. Abigail came across this and sent it to her husband through the mail.

> Above the mists of mouldering Time
> Thy Fame, O Adams, soars sublime
> Who first the British Lion spurn'd
> And gave the Terms when Peace return'd.

Like Washington writing to those who named their children after him, Adams also felt that he should acknowledge the regard of others. "Deeply touched by the patriotic addresses that kept pouring in," says biographer David McCullough, "he spent hours laboring to answer them, as if obliged to respond to each and every one." Sometimes he overreacted, responding too effusively to praise that was modest at best, which is the way of a man who expects the worst and then suddenly finds himself meeting with show after show of approval.

Yet the approval was never enough for Adams — never loud enough, precise enough, or lasting enough. Not because he had an ego so large it needed constant feeding, but for precisely the opposite reason. His ego was in many ways a small one, and doubt and resentment plagued him. Perhaps his ego *did* need feeding, but only to reach normal proportions.

His wife did as much as she could. Abigail Adams was one of the era's most remarkable women — bold, intelligent, perceptive in matters both political and personal. Adams never made an important decision without consulting her, and when she and her husband were separated because of his government service, which was often, she kept the bonds between them strong by writing him scores of eloquent letters, raising both his spirits and her own in times of trial.

In one of her letters, when she was in Massachusetts and he in Philadelphia as Washington's vice president — not only the first man to hold the office but the first to experience its uselessness — she told him of her love and encouraged him to keep his eyes on the future, when more successes would surely come if he continued to strive for them, continued to keep the flame burning that had first been lit in his days as a student in James Putnam's care. She told him: "Our attachment to Character, Reputation, and Fame increases, I believe, with our Years." Note that Abigail places fame in good company. Note also that, unlike her husband, she capitalizes the word.

Alexander Hamilton, born on the West Indian island of Nevis in 1755, was the only one of the Founding Fathers who did not spend his early years in America. He was also the only one born out of wedlock and, perhaps even more than Franklin, the most financially straitened as a young man. His father had deserted the family without marrying his mother, his mother died when he was thirteen, and the cousins with whom he was then sent to live also died, barely more than boys themselves. To dream of survival was courageous. To escape from Nevis and succeed in the colonies was as unrealistic a fantasy in which a child in his circumstances could possibly have indulged. Yet fantasize he did, and through will, ability, and — on more than one occasion — sheer audacity, taking every rejection as a further incentive, he made himself a famous man.

Hamilton first became known during the Revolutionary War, a few years after arriving in America, where he impressed enough people with his scholarship and passion to be recommended to George Washington as an aide. Washington met the young man and, also impressed, took him on as a secretary. Hamilton started out by tending to correspondence and organizing paperwork for the general's command. It was not stimulating work, but Hamilton applied himself to it with diligence and without complaint.

Soon, however, he showed abilities far beyond those that such simple chores demanded, and he quickly became Washington's most trusted adviser on matters both military and political. Washington wouldn't go into battle or even communicate with government officials about the needs of his army without first consulting Hamilton, and Hamilton usually replied with acumen far beyond his age and experience.

He also began to write Washington's speeches, as well as some of his correspondence, and, rising to the rank of lieutenant colonel, he occasionally led troops into battle. He did so wisely, achieving his objectives with maximum efficiency and a minimum of casualties — but not enough to suit him. Hamilton yearned for the military life during the war, not administration, and he constantly asked Washington to give him more opportunities in the field.

After the war, Hamilton studied law and served two years in Congress, representing New York. He attended the Constitutional Convention at Washington's side, once again providing counsel that Washington found indispensable. He also provided that counsel to others, whether they wanted it or not. He seemed too young to know all that he knew, and too confident by far in sharing his knowledge with others.

After the Constitution was agreed upon by the delegates, Hamilton worked tirelessly for its passage. He joined James Madison and John Jay in writing the Federalist Papers, a series of eighty-five letters initially published in the *New York Independent Journal* and then reprinted in almost every other newspaper in the country. They are a remarkable collection of essays, philosophy more than journalism, and Hamilton wrote fifty-one of the pieces himself.

The purpose of the letters, Hamilton stated in the introduction to the first, was to persuade New York to ratify the Constitution, insisting that it "will add the inducements of philanthropy to those of patriotism, to heighten the solicitude which all considerate and good men must feel for the event." But the letters served the larger goal of explaining to all Americans how at least some of the founders believed the Constitution should be interpreted and applied. They acted as annotations to the Constitution by three of the most learned minds of the time, all of whom had contributed significantly to the document in the first place.

And yet in one of the letters, Hamilton digresses to make the case for fame, which he defines as "the ruling passion of the noblest minds, which would prompt a man to plan and undertake extensive and arduous enterprises for the public benefit, requiring considerable time to mature and perfect them, if he could flatter himself with the prospect of being allowed to finish what he had begun." About Aaron Burr, who became both Hamilton's enemy and murderer, Hamilton could think of few things more scathing to say than that he "never appeared solicitous for fame."

The same could not be said of the man who stood at the receiving end of Burr's bullet less than four years later.

It took more than just the Federalist Papers to persuade New Yorkers to ratify the Constitution. Hamilton lobbied, cajoled, persuaded, and on one occasion even threatened, claiming that if the state did not give its approval to the plan for a national government, New York City, which favored the plan, would secede, forming a political entity of its own and throwing the United States into turmoil.

The state of New York finally did ratify, although with the smallest margin of acceptance in any of the states — three votes. Deservedly, Hamilton received much of the credit. His name appeared in the newspapers as the principal force behind ratification, and crowds parading through the streets of Manhattan chanted his name, cheering the paperwork that had established the new country. "So exuberant was the lionization of Alexander Hamilton," writes biographer Ron Chernow, "that admirers wanted to rechristen the city 'Hamiltonia.' It was one of the few times in his life that Hamilton basked in the warmth of public adulation."

He had long since achieved his goal of attracting notice; he had seen to that in the Revolutionary War. But fame, and the antagonism it seemed to draw, frustrated him. Many of his ideas for fiscal reform and trade policy were not implemented until after his death, and even those that were accepted in his lifetime, such as his proposal that the federal government assume the debts the states had incurred during the war, came about only after struggles that left Hamilton bitter and depressed, and his critics no less bitter in their denunciations of him and depressed that his ideas had prevailed. When Hamilton announced plans for a national banking system and a mint for the production and regulation of currency, critics accused him of trying to invest the central government with the powers of a monarchy, and advocates of states' rights attacked him as if he were an armed invader.

He was probably not consoled in 1791 when he heard from his friend Fisher Ames in Boston that his fame had reached new heights. "We have you exhibited here in Wax," Ames reported, after having attended the opening of a new museum. "You see that they are resolved to get money from you in every form."

The founding fathers, in the words of Arthur Schlesinger Sr., were "the most remarkable generation of public men in the history of the United States or perhaps any other nation." They were famous men who deserved their fame because of the high-mindedness of their goals and their zeal in pursuing them and for what they achieved as a result. At least in the mythic sense of the term, however, they cannot be called heroes — and the distinctions are intriguing ones, not only for what they tell us about the men themselves, but for what they tell us about the nation these men so carefully constructed.

In *Heroes: A History of Hero Worship*, Lucy Hughes-Hallett defines her topic in a number of ways, all of which exclude the subjects of the present volume. For instance, she writes that "hero worship is the cult of the individual, and the hero is always imagined standing alone."

In our imagination, the founders do not stand alone, except in such unheroic settings as farms, offices, or studies. But this is not where we normally see them. We see Washington at the head of his soldiers and later at the head of the national government, the clear superior of his associates but just as obviously a part of them. We see Franklin in the company of his fellow printers, scientists, philosophers, statesmen, and any number of admirers in Parisian salons or on the streets of Philadelphia, the man around whom all others have arrayed themselves. Jefferson, Adams, and Hamilton are perhaps more solitary figures, but not in the way that Hughes-Hallett describes her heroes, and even in their unaccompanied moments we envision them sitting at their desks and working for their fellow citizens, ensuring the welfare of all rather than plotting their own advancement.

"Heroes expose themselves to mortal danger in pursuit of immortality," Hughes-Hallett says of Homer's Achilles, who is to her "one of the wild ones," a man with a "readiness to risk his own death." But among the founders, only Washington and (to a lesser extent) Hamilton were fighting men, and neither took unnecessary risks or behaved recklessly on the battlefield to attain a more illustrious name. The others were men of thought more than deed, hoping to gain the esteem of both their generation and those to follow through the consequences of their ideas. They did not behave recklessly even in legislative chambers.

Nor were Washington and Hamilton contemptuous of civilian authority, as Hughes-Hallett finds that heroes invariably are. Washington might have bristled at Congress's sluggishness in acceding to his wartime requests for men, materiel, and payment, but he never denied, or tried to subvert, the congressional right to make decisions. And Hamilton learned from his superior officer.

The Spanish hero Rodrigo Diaz de Vivar, whom we know as El Cid, once deposited his wife and child at a monastery before heading off to battle, and Hughes-Hallett refers to his "turning his back on the feminine sphere of sex and family in order to embark upon his great adventure in proper heroic fashion, unencumbered and alone."

The founders never turned their backs on family. To them, the support of loved ones was indispensable, no matter what the endeavor. Benjamin Franklin, whose wife did not accompany him to France, who probably preferred that the two of them live on different continents rather than in the same house, and who often partook of the company of other women while abroad, wrote often to his wife. He sent her advice about the rearing of the children and the maintenance of the household and assured her of his continuing affection, albeit largely platonic. When she died, having seen little of him during their marriage, he did not return to America for the funeral. It was a decision he did not make painlessly.

Adams was also separated from his wife while in France, but his heart ached for her and hers for him, and the volumes of correspondence that passed between them are the most poignant love letters of the time. Hamilton had an unfortunate and well-publicized affair with a woman who then conspired with her husband to blackmail him. Otherwise his devotion to his wife seems to have been constant, and his shame for the liaison was an enduring burden. Jefferson's wife died when he was thirty-nine and they had been married only ten years. Among the ways he coped with her loss — in addition to his affair with Maria Cosway and his later relationship with his slave Sally Hemings — was an extreme devotion to his daughters. He fretted over their education, their manners, and especially their suitors, playing the roles of mother and father to his girls and finding enrichment in both. Washington had no children of his own, but was as devoted to his wife's children as he was to Martha herself.

These were not men who saw the feminine sphere as an encumbrance, who wanted to fight their battles, political or otherwise, alone.

Hughes-Hallett continues: "Historical heroes, whose hero status depends at least in part on the public's identification of them with legendary counterparts, have frequently been people with no fixed position in the society which expected such great things of them." The Founding Fathers had no legendary counterparts; they were originals who, for this reason, were able to create a nation that was itself original. In addition, they were men of fixed position. Often the positions changed, but with the exception of journalist Sam Adams, they all held public office of one sort or another at the time of their greatest successes. And they did not assume their fixed positions by force, the usual method of the hero, but by the carefully cultivated consent of their fellows.

As did Hughes-Hallett, the nineteenth-century British historian and essayist Thomas Carlyle produced a volume on heroism, and she quotes him as defining a hero as "a man with an almost mythical awareness of what needed to be done." The founders, on occasion, didn't even have a mortal awareness of what needed to be done. They were puzzled, frustrated, often uncertain of the proper path. Washington struggled with his military decisions and sometimes made the wrong ones. The others, with the exception of Hamilton, did not believe themselves omniscient, and were constantly assembling in committees, congresses, and conventions, debating the proper course of action more than insisting on their own notions, always eager to take into account the opinions and experiences of others, always placing a premium on consensus, no matter how much time or effort was required to achieve it.

And, says Hughes-Hallett, "a hero must be able either to seduce or intimidate: either way he needs an outsize personality and a talent for projecting it." Franklin, whose personality was outgoing rather than outsize, came as close as any of the founders to meeting this criterion, but not close enough to qualify. Biographer Willard Sterne Randall says of Hamilton that he had an "overall avidity and brightness that created the aura of a charismatic figure," but he could be standoffish at times, coldly distracted, giving the impression that his mind was on business, not on those whose company he was keeping. Washington was sometimes withdrawn. Adams lacked personality, although he was capable now and then of spurts in which he demonstrated both warmth and a selfless concern for others. Jefferson is best described as restrained, although some found him shy, and James Madison, who succeeded Jefferson as president, can barely be described at all. On occasions when they needed to seduce or intimidate, these men relied on what they believed to be the strength of their arguments rather than their flair in delivering them.

To say, then, that the Founding Fathers were famous rather than heroic is not to take issue with Schlesinger; it is, rather, to praise the founders for the communality of their vision, the breadth of their insight, and the humility of their actions. Heroes, as Hughes-Hallett shows in her book, are as likely to be traitors as patriots, as likely to wreak havoc as to build civilizations.

The founders sought a kind of fame we do not know today. They sought it through behavior seldom exhibited anymore, and even less often brought to public attention by media outlets attracted to freakishness and violence more than civic benefaction. And they sought it because they were at the same time pursuing a goal to which they had been inspired, at least in part, by the Roman republic: a nation that would provide the greatest good and the most opportunity for as many of its citizens as possible.

Part II

The Ingredients of Renown

Chapter 4
Ambition

IF FAME WAS AN END FOR THE FOUNDING FATHERS, ambition was the means. Even Washington and Jefferson, among the least driven of the men who made America, were eager to publicize their names and control their reputations.

Although he was often forced to live elsewhere, Washington constantly longed for Mount Vernon. He wrote of these feelings to his wife Martha and discussed them with associates at the end of another long day on the battlefield or in the meeting hall. Jefferson was equally wistful about Monticello. The two men returned as often as they could to homes so important that they seemed to be extensions of them — and then they wrote to friends of their contentment at being once again situated within familiar walls.

But when asked to return to the corridors of power, Washington and Jefferson always answered in the affirmative. A sense of duty more than a lust for glory motivated them, but at the same time they could not help but feel the twinge of what Leo Braudy has so deftly referred to as "civic narcissism."

When leading his troops in both the French and Indian and Revolutionary wars, Washington spoke often of ambition. In most cases, he was trying to encourage it in others for military ends rather than describing his own for personal gain. Addressing his soldiers during the French and Indian War, he preached "that laudable Ambition of serving Our Country, and meriting its applause." In the later war, urging his officers to set a proper example for those serving under them, he said, "It would be a happy pride, and a most laudable ambition, to see the commanding officers of corps vieing with each other in discipline and good behavior." Washington wanted the applause for his men no less than he wanted it for himself.

On those occasions when Washington spoke of his own ambition, it was always with humility, and always in relation to the duties that occupied him at the time. When the Revolutionary War was a year old and he received a letter from the Continental Congress congratulating him on forcing British troops out of Boston, he replied that "it will ever be my highest ambition to approve myself a faithful Servant of the Public; and that, to be in any degree instrumental in procuring to my American Brethren a restitution of their just rights and Privileges, will constitute my chief happiness."

Many years later, James Madison wrote to a friend about Washington's attitude, how important it had been not only to the morale of his troops, but to the outcome of the war: "I have always believed that if General Washington had yielded to a usurping ambition, he would have found an insuperable obstacle in the incorruptibility of a sufficient portion of those under his command, and that the exalted praise due to him & them, was derived not from a forbearance to effect a revolution within their power, but from a love of liberty and of country, which there was abundant reason to believe, no facility of success could have seduced."

Some of Washington's biographers believe that his ambition ran deeper. Joseph J. Ellis declares that, even as a young man, Washington was displaying a "combination of bottomless ambition and the near obsession with self-control." And as an older man there is no doubt that ambition flared in him when his competence and leadership were under challenge.

James Thomas Flexner, however, presents a more nuanced view, distinguishing between different kinds of ambition as he writes perceptively of Washington's return to Mount Vernon when the fighting against the British had ended: "With the vanishing of the winter snows and the loosening of his own almost murderous exhaustion, Washington exploded into perpetual motion. However, all this activity was for him quiet. As he himself explained it, the multitudinous details of his military life, which affected the lives of men and the destiny of nations (to say nothing of his own reputation) had kept his mind disagreeably 'on the stretch.' By contrast, the business of retirement kept his mind 'agreeably amused.'"

Flexner concludes, in other words, that Washington's ambition — at least at certain times in his life — was not for fame as a public man so much as it was for utility in his private life as the manager of his lands and the caretaker of his crops and animals. That is to say, he wanted to succeed at the quotidian rather than the extraordinary.

A few years later, of course, Washington's agreeable amusement came to an end. He would be stretched as he had never been stretched before, leaving behind the life of gentleman farmer to become president of the Constitutional Convention and then serving two terms as the first president of the nation that the Constitution had produced. It might not have been his ambition to do either — not ambition in the single-minded, stomach-churning, full-blooded sense of the word — but he knew that chief executive of the United States of America was a position only he could fill. Duty again. He did not seek the position for selfish reasons, but neither did he shrink from its rewards.

Jefferson couldn't make up his mind about ambition, either. As the Revolutionary War was coming to a close, Jefferson looked back on the hardships it had brought and the contributions he believed he had made to its successful outcome. "To merit the Approbation of good and virtuous Men," he wrote, "is the height of my ambition, and will be a full compensation for all my toils and Sufferings in the long and painful Contest we have been engaged."

Still, he didn't allow himself to endorse a conscious striving for fame. He could never quite decide whether ambition was the natural craving of the talented individual to be noticed, or the aberrant impulse of the mediocre fellow who wanted to seem more accomplished than he really was.

In 1794, after resigning as Washington's secretary of state and moving back to Monticello, Jefferson behaved like someone who would never again depart, who, like Washington, wanted nothing more of his days than the business of retirement. He planted and tended herbs and vegetables. He set up a small factory there and manufactured and sold nails. He read and entertained, keeping both his library and his wine cellar well stocked. He wrote to friends — but not often. He was enjoying himself too much to maintain an active correspondence, and a few of his acquaintances drifted away with the inattention. And he began to remodel and enlarge Monticello, his work-in-progress that never seemed to make as much progress as he had hoped. That he was content in what he thought of as his self-imposed exile from public life is obvious. He had been witness to enough tumult for a lifetime, he believed. He had been the subject of enough controversy to leave him pining for smooth waters for the rest of his life.

One of the people with whom he did continue to correspond was Madison, and he wrote to him at the time, "The little spice of ambition which I had in my younger days has long since evaporated, and I set still less store by a posthumous than present name." A few months later, he would repeat the theme to John Adams, telling him, "I have no ambition to govern men. It is a painful and thankless office." And then one imagines Jefferson setting down his pen to stroll outside and look in on his factory, make sure his lands were being properly cared for, and take deep breaths of the sweet-scented country air that meant so much to him. It didn't last.

The next year Jefferson ran for president. Finishing second to Adams, he became vice president. Four years later he ran for president again and won, acquitting himself admirably in the midst of a new batch of controversy. Expansion, threats of war, and outbreaks of piracy filled his two terms as chief executive — and all eyes were on him all the time.

His own eyes, when he closed them, were on Monticello.

Alexander Hamilton *did* admit to the tug of ambition. It proved too powerful a force for him either to gainsay or ignore. Even as a child in the West Indies, he was writing to his friend Edward Stevens, a college student in New York, "to confess my weakness." He explained, "my ambition is [so] prevalent that I contemn the groveling condition of a clerk or the like, to which my Fortune &c. condemns me, and would willingly risk my life though not my character to exalt my Station. I am confident, Ned, that my youth excludes me from any hopes of immediate preferment nor do I desire it, but I mean to prepare the way for futurity." Hamilton's ambition was of a very different sort from Jefferson's, and the difference was succinctly expressed one night with John Adams in attendance to overhear the exchange.

The year was 1791, almost a decade after the colonists and the British had ceased hostilities, but for many Americans it was not a time of peace. Natives were attacking them in their settlements in Ohio and other parts of the Northwest Territory. The seat of their national government had moved recently from New York to Philadelphia. Vermont was about to become the fourteenth state and would join the others in deciding whether to ratify the Bill of Rights. Samuel Slater had built a steam-powered machine to process cotton, which was about to revolutionize the country's cotton output. It was the beginning of the Industrial Revolution in America.

Abroad, the French were marching closer to a republic, with the National Assembly having drafted a constitution that called for a limited monarchy and a unicameral legislature whose members would be elected by popular, if restricted, vote.

With these recent events in the air, Hamilton, Jefferson, and Adams met over dinner to discuss the more pressing issues of governance in the absence of the head of state, President Washington, who had recently departed from Philadelphia to make a tour of the South. But that wasn't the only topic at hand, as summarized by historian Douglass Adair:

> "After the cloth was removed," Jefferson reports, "and our question agreed and dismissed, conversation began on other matters. ...The room being hung around with a collection of portraits of remarkable men, among them those of [Sir Francis] Bacon, Newton, and Locke, Hamilton asked me who they were. I told him they were my *trinity* of the *three greatest men* the world had ever produced, naming them. He [Hamilton] paused for some time. 'The greatest man,' he said, 'that ever lived, was Julius Caesar.' "

Jefferson's ambitions, in other words, tended to be intellectual. Hamilton's were more dynamic. Jefferson wanted to be known for his mastery of thought. Hamilton, at least in Jefferson's view, sought the mastery of men and institutions, by military might if necessary. Hamilton's kind of ambition is the more likely to attract the notice of historians — if not alter the course of history. Ron Chernow calls it a "vaulting ambition." The clergyman Hugh Knox, who knew Hamilton at an early age, saw in him even then "an ambition to excel."

Many years later, Washington agreed. "That he is ambitious I readily grant," Washington said of Hamilton, but went on to defend his behavior as being "of that laudable kind which prompts a man to excel in whatever he takes in hand."

Sometimes, though, it prompts a man to be a pest. During the war, when Hamilton was constantly imploring Washington for more battle duty, Washington usually responded by telling him he was too valuable a confidant and strategist to expose to the enemy's muskets. It was rejection by praise, and Hamilton hated it. He kept asking. Washington kept turning him down. And so it went, back and forth, whenever another confrontation with the British loomed and Hamilton thought his superior officer had the patience to hear one more plea.

Once, when the two men were temporarily separated and Hamilton was desperate for a joint command with the Marquis de Lafayette in a charge against the British in New York, Hamilton wrote to Washington at length. "Sometime last fall," he began, "when I spoke to your Excellency about going to the southward, I explained to you candidly my feelings with respect to military reputation, and how much it was my object to act a conspicuous part in some enterprise that might perhaps raise my character as a soldier above mediocrity." Hamilton wanted Washington to give him that opportunity now, "to avoid the embarrassment" of having to explain to others why he had been bypassed.

On this occasion, Washington seems seriously to have considered Hamilton's request. For strategic reasons, however, the New York mission had to be canceled. Washington explained the reasons to Hamilton, and Hamilton told the boss he understood. Then, after a decent interval, he suggested to Washington that another command might be in order. This time he got it. Washington put him at the head of a light infantry battalion that fought at Yorktown, the Revolutionary War's most decisive battle. "The desire for reward," Hamilton said, "is one of the strongest incentives for human conduct."

While humble beginnings and an aggressive temperament fueled Hamilton, insecurity motivated John Adams. "The first way for a young man to set himself on the road toward glorious reputation,"

Cicero wrote, "is to win renown," and Adams took to the road in earnest, especially during his first few years as a lawyer. Adams knew he would have to work long hours under James Putnam's tutelage. When ennui set in, he would work longer still, outrunning his boredom. When he fell into a not uncommon depression, when "he imagined . . . that posterity would hardly remember his name," he pushed himself beyond the limits of endurance, achieving levels of dedication and concentration that scarcely seemed possible to others. And when all else failed, when it seemed that he would not make a name for himself no matter what he did, when he feared that no animating occasion would ever call forth his powers, he subjected himself to the indignities of self-promotion: an occasional toot of his own horn, an occasional blare. He wanted to be more than important, more than a public figure; he wanted to be indispensable.

It was a long time before John Adams dreamed of a haven like Mount Vernon or Monticello and a time when people were not calling out his name, demanding assistance that only he could provide.

Benjamin Franklin might have been the oldest of the founders, but he was also the freest spirit, the least troubled soul, the most distinctive, in many ways the most distinguished of all the men of his generation — and, at least to outward appearances, the least concerned with ambition. He did not lack it, nor was he ignorant of its consequences. Before he soured on the British, some thought he wanted to become the first royal governor of Pennsylvania or to hold some other important position under the Crown's aegis.

But ambition came so naturally to Franklin, was such an integral part of his personality, such a logical outgrowth of it, that it didn't seem to him a matter worthy of contemplation. It was an instinct more than a strategy.

Franklin didn't educate himself for a successful career, which would have been ambitious in the conventional sense. Rather, he educated himself because learning was a joy to him, and he wanted to feel that joy as deeply as he could, expressing it to others, asking for and refuting information, always with the goal of adding to his storehouse of fact and learned opinion.

Franklin didn't invent the armonica, bifocals, the Franklin stove, the lightning rod, the storage battery, and swim fins to impress others and amass a fortune. Instead, he invented because of the satisfaction of solving problems whose solutions had not only escaped others but would benefit others, too, and the further satisfaction of sharing his devices and the reasoning behind them with all who wanted to know and had tried to work out similar problems before. Again: to add to mankind's storehouse of fact and learned opinion.

Franklin didn't experiment with electricity, magnetism, and refrigeration to earn a place in the pantheon of world scientists — another example of conventional ambition. He experimented because of the thrill of discovery, and he could not help but show off those discoveries, to discuss them with people of similar interests, and to encourage them to make use of his theories and move beyond them. The progress of science mattered more to him than his personal gratification. He was effusive, tireless, but not premeditated enough to be called ambitious. He was who he was: a uniquely gifted and voluble human being. He could be introspective at times, but there was so much else to pique his interest, demand his energy, reward his devotion — so much other than himself, outside himself. Introspection may well have seemed to him a form of selfishness.

Franklin's accomplishments, combined with his ebullient nature, could not help but make him famous. He might have seemed full of himself at times, but he was brimming with perceptions of the world around him and did not need to be consciously ambitious to enlarge his name.

But there is something puzzling here — perhaps even hypocritical. Although the founders thought fame a virtue, they hesitated to admit their desire for it. It was as if public attention were the woman they wanted to marry and ambition the process of courtship. For a man to be seen walking down the aisle with his bride on his arm was to display himself in the most dignified of settings. To be seen at an earlier stage, pounding on her door, demanding admittance to proclaim his devotion yet again — this was something else altogether, aggressive at the least and probably uncouth.

What if his suit were rejected? He would look the fool. What if those who learned of it found it audacious, the lady too far above his station? He would look like a social climber. What if his suit became the subject of idle speculation, devalued because of the casual manner in which others discussed it? He would be dismissed as common. Remember: this was an era that valued discretion. You did not make public announcements of urges that were inherently personal.

John Adams once revealed that his cousin Sam had been asked to draw up a blueprint for government in Boston, and that he was reluctant to do so. "He told me," John wrote, "that he felt an Ambition, which was very apt to mislead a Man, that of doing something extraordinary and he wanted to consult a friend who might suggest some thoughts to mind."

John was the right friend, and not just because of the family tie. He had thought much about ambition, and despite possessing more than his share — or perhaps *because* he did — he claimed a certain wariness. In a letter to Abigail in 1777, he stated, and probably even believed, that "Of that Ambition which has Power for its Object, I dont believe I have a Spark in my Heart. . . . There are other Kinds of Ambition of which I have a great deal." What kinds? He answered the question in another letter a few months later. "Let us have Ambition enough to keep our Simplicity, or Frugality and our Integrity, and transmit these Virtues as the fairest of Inheritances to our Children."

Benjamin Franklin might not have been one to reflect on, or even notice, his own ambition, but he was dismayed at the way the quality revealed itself in others. "Is it possible that Men abounding with all the necessaries of Life can flatter or Cringe to gratifie little impulses of Ambition and gain imaginary Applause. No[t] if endued with a small degree of my Spirit for I think his Condition who enjoys Affluence and releases any share his reason and honestly to purchase Fame is more contemptable than the most abject Patient in our Hospital and deserves less Pity."

To newspapers that opposed his presidential candidacy in 1800, Jefferson was seen as contemptible for a number of reasons, among them that he was a man of "insatiable ambition," by which the paper meant that he wanted more than he deserved, and cared more for himself than for those he would represent. It was a serious charge, possibly enough to keep some men from voting for him and certainly enough to raise doubts among many others.

Even Alexander Hamilton — who flashed his ambition as a courtier in Europe might flash bejeweled fingers — denied ambition when he feared he might be going too far. After one of Washington's many refusals to send him into battle, he tried to persuade the general that the matter was not of great importance to him after all. "These are my pretensions, at this advanced period of the war," he wrote to his commander, "to be employed in the only way, which my situation admits. . . . I am incapable of wishing to obtain any object by importunity." The truth, of course, was that Hamilton was incapable of *not* importuning when he wanted something badly enough, and of stewing interminably when he was denied. But he realized that proper etiquette sometimes requires demurral, however insincere.

And although Hamilton gave his blessing to fame in one article of the Federalist Papers, he warned against ambition in eight of them. Perhaps he thought he could rid himself of ambition's curses simply by denouncing them in print. He wrote about "perverted ambition," about the "assaults of ambition" on liberty, about "the ambition or enmity of other nations," about men who are "ambitious, vindictive, and rapacious." In other letters, he showed no less disregard for it, referring to "ambition and jealousy" in two of the essays, calling forth the evils of "ambition or revenge" in another, and in still another expressing the fear that the "sacred knot which binds the people of America together [might] be severed or dissolved by ambition or by avarice, by jealousy or by misrepresentation."

And it wasn't just Hamilton. Other founders also decried ambition, thinking it a sin, unable to reconcile the terrible contradiction that the path to virtuous fame led through so egregious a vice as the yearning for it.

Adams warned that, no matter how a person tried to control it, ambition "at last takes possession of the whole soul so absolutely, that a man sees nothing in the world of importance to others or himself, but in his object." On another occasion, he shook his fists at "the horrid Figures of Jealousy Envy, Hatred Revenge, Vanity Ambition, Avarice Treachery, Tyranny Insolence."

Washington denounced "lawless ambition, rapine and devastation," "the mercenary instruments of ambition," and "the folly and madness of unbounded ambition." Madison railed against "ambition & intrigues," "ambition & self-Interest," "ambition or corruption," and "greedy ambition."

Even Patrick Henry took up the cry. He joined the others in making ambition the partner of avarice in a letter to a friend and in another letter praised Americans for being "this happy people," while at the same time claiming that the nations of Europe were "precipitated by the rage of ambition or folly, in the pursuit of the most magnificent projects," and that as a consequence, they had "riveted the fetters of bondage on themselves and their descendants."

In one case, however, Henry's own ambition exceeded folly. It vaulted all the way to deceit. It was an incident known as the Parson's Cause, and without it Henry would probably be far less known and venerated than he is today.

Although it is one of the curses of the twenty-first century, tobacco was the salvation of the British colonial experiment along the Atlantic coast, the first cash crop in the first permanent settlement of Englishmen in the New World.

Jamestown was founded in 1607 in what is now Virginia, but for the first several years of its existence the settlers couldn't figure out a way to support themselves. They tried corn, timber, glassblowing, even silkworms. Nothing worked; Jamestown grew more and more impoverished, failing to attract new settlers in significant numbers, and it drained more of the motherland's resources with each passing year.

Then, in 1617, John Rolfe — best known to history as the husband of Pocahontas — developed a strain of tobacco that was something of a miracle. After experimenting for several years, every trial an error, Rolfe came up with *Nicotiana tabacum*, which was hardy enough to thrive in the Virginia soil and yet mild enough to please even the most delicate of palates among British smokers. Suddenly Jamestown had an industry, a reason for being. Tobacco became the first profitable American export — and not a moment too soon. James I, the English monarch after whom Jamestown was named, had long been frustrated with his eponymous colony. Had it continued to flounder, the king might well have given up on the notion of settling North America, or at least that particular part of it. The Englishmen already there would return home or scatter inland, to be replaced in time by colonists from France, Spain, or Portugal. The history of the United States would have been written in ways that no one could have foreseen. Tobacco eliminated any such possibility.

Soon the leaf became big business not only for Virginia but for neighboring colonies as well, colonies that had adopted the Rolfe formula and were growing their own *Nicotiana tabacum*. And then it became more than a business, not just a product in itself but a standard for measuring the value of other products. Which is to say, tobacco became a form of currency. Almost everything that could be purchased with cash in seventeenth-century America could also be purchased with tobacco, from slaves to wives, from a blacksmith's labor to a militiaman's vigilance. You could use tobacco to buy food, beverages, fabrics, tools, and books — even the Bible. In the years leading up to the Revolutionary War, churchgoers in Virginia paid their clergymen in tobacco. As the historian Jerome E. Brooks has observed, "Superb sermons were often thundered from pulpits on the importance of raising good tobacco and the moral necessity of curing it properly."

The thunderers were paid about 16,000 pounds of tobacco a year, although they could supplement their earnings with extra duties — another 200 pounds for officiating at a wedding, perhaps twice that for some well-chosen words at a funeral. Most clerics did not think it enough. Most farmers thought it excessive. Tensions simmered between parson and parishioner from the outset, and they increased as time went on and the quality of the crops varied. There seemed to be no way of resolving the situation — until nature forced the issue.

In 1755, it stopped raining in Virginia. Just stopped. For days, then weeks, then months, not so much as a single drop or a damp breeze. It was one of the worst droughts the colony had ever suffered, and it resulted in the poorest tobacco crop in living memory. Farmers had to notify the clergy that they would not receive their usual stipends this year.

And then they began to think about the future. What if the drought continued? What if next year was as bad as this? Even if it wasn't, the farmers would still be suffering from this year's losses and might be suffering from them for years to come. Would their preachers expect 16,000 pounds of leaf regardless? The risks of agriculture were great, and the planters thought they should not have to assume them alone.

The Virginia Assembly agreed, but it took a while. In 1758, it gave tobacco farmers the relief they had long sought in the form of the Two-Penny Act, which, for the time being, allowed all debts incurred in tobacco, including the salaries of clergymen, to be paid off at the rate of two pence per pound of leaf. It was a tremendous savings for the farmers, and they rejoiced at the news. The clerics thought the devil had entered the assembly and cast the deciding votes.

The clergymen insisted that they were not being greedy They understood they could not expect their full 16,000 pounds in a bad year. But bad years, they maintained, were hardly the norm. Tobacco production had, in fact, increased dramatically since the drought in 1755. Why, the preachers asked, was the assembly addressing a problem that nature had already resolved? Why should those farmers who had fallen behind in their payments be allowed to fall even further behind despite the fact that they were once again prospering? Was the eternal life of the soul not, in the long run, more important than agricultural profit? If so, why were the providers of salvation being asked to supply it at a discount?

Virginia's men of God asked their legislators to reconsider the Two-Penny Act. The legislators refused, but the act had a built-in expiration date of one year, and the clerics, virtually all members of the Church of England, decided to go over the assembly's head and appeal to their fellow Anglicans in Parliament not to allow the act to be extended. The strategy worked. They were assured that the act would expire as scheduled no matter what colonial lawmakers decided.

More important, Parliament ruled that preachers who had lost income because of the act were entitled to back pay for the year that it had been in existence. It was more of a victory for the men of the cloth than they had thought possible, and many of them were quick to hire lawyers and file suits. The Parson's Cause was their attempt to get the money that they believed was owed to them for services so devoutly rendered.

Unlike John Adams, Patrick Henry was not highly regarded as a lawyer. In fact, Jefferson told biographer William Wirt that Henry's knowledge of the law in his early days was "not worth a copper."

The opinion was seconded, in gentler language, by the panel of examiners who voted in 1760 that Henry was not yet qualified to practice. And they probably would have counted him similarly unqualified in 1763, when the Reverend James Maury sought justice in the third of the Parson's Cause cases to come to trial. Henry did not serve as Maury's attorney at first, though his father, Colonel John Henry, was coincidentally the presiding judge.

Maury was not optimistic about his chances. He thought the jury had been stacked against him, that its members were not only farmers who opposed additional payments of tobacco to ministers in principle but also, more to his detriment, Protestants who bore a deep resentment against Maury's Anglican preachings. Judge Henry was a loyal Anglican, having baptized his son in the faith, but Maury didn't think that would count for much.

The trial was brief. Judge Henry allowed both sides to have their say, and they said it quickly. By now the issues were clear to all. The jury retired to deliberate, but not for long. To Maury's astonishment, and to the surprise of virtually everyone else in the courtroom, as well as those who learned of the verdict later, the jurors filed back to their seats after no more than an hour to announce that they had ruled in the cleric's favor. Maury was entitled to a certain quantity of tobacco under the terms of the Two-Penny Act, and a second trial was scheduled to determine exactly how much he would receive.

There are different accounts of what happened next. According to one, John Lewis, the counsel for Maury's parishioners, was so disgusted with the decision that he cursed both judge and jury, railing at their ineptitude and unfairness and then resigning, refusing to represent the farmers at the second trial, refusing to argue on behalf of limiting the payment to Maury when he believed that Maury deserved not so much as a single leaf in the first place. According to another version, Lewis stepped aside because, having lost the first trial, he thought another lawyer would better serve his client's interests in the next one.

Either way, the farmers had to find a replacement for Lewis — and fast. They didn't have time to look for the most qualified candidate, and even if they had had the time, they didn't have the money to pay him. Pooling all the cash they could dig out of their pockets and taking into account all they had at home, they determined that they could afford no more than fifteen shillings, which would not attract a lawyer of high caliber and perhaps not even one who was competent.

Enter Patrick Henry, the very personification of a bargain, a man less interested in the compensation he would receive than in the attention the case was now attracting because of its unexpected verdict. Henry was a surprising choice to represent the defendants not just because of his background, but because his father was presiding over the second trial just as he had the first. Some believed that this would give young Henry a decided advantage. Others believed the judge wasn't as enamored with his son as he might have been and wanted to teach the young firebrand a lesson. Maury's parishioners didn't have time to fret about either. Henry was their man, fifteen shillings the rate.

As the second trial began, Henry saw the opportunity he had long been awaiting to make a name for himself. He did not, however, start out well. As he began to explain why Maury should be awarded no more than a pittance in judgment, he seemed uncertain. His voice was low, his manner diffident, and his gestures halting. He did not meet the eyes of the jurors, did not seem to engage them.

But he quickly gained confidence and momentum, and began to soar into realms of verbal excess uncommon even by the theatrical standards of his profession. The king of England, Henry told the jury, by failing to support a longer lifespan for the Two-Penny Act, "from being the father of his people, degenerates into a Tyrant, and forfeits all right to his subjects' obedience." As for Maury and his fellow servants of God:

> We have heard a great deal about the benevolence and holy zeal of our reverend clergy, but how is this manifested? Do they manifest their zeal in the cause of religion and humanity by

practicing the mild and benevolent precepts of the Gospel of Jesus? Do they feed the hungry and clothe the naked? Oh, no, gentlemen! Instead of feeding the hungry and clothing the naked, these rapacious harpies would, were their powers equal to their will, snatch from the hearth of their honest parishioner his last hoecake, from the widow and her orphan children their last milch cow! The last bed, nay the last blanket from the lying-in woman!

It was not just verbal excess, it was verbal savagery. Incensed, Maury's attorney rose to his feet. "The gentleman has spoken treason," he is reported to have cried, especially in his comments about George III. A few others in the audience repeated the charge: "Treason, treason, treason" — a menacing chant.

But not everyone agreed. One of Henry's biographers, Richard R. Beeman, says that as Henry ranted on, the members of the jury and virtually everyone else who heard him were "taken captive; and [were] so delighted with their captivity, that they followed implicitly, whithersoever he led them; that at his bidding their tears flowed from pity, and their cheeks flushed with indignation; that when it was over, they felt as if they had just been awaked from some ecstatic dream, of which they were unable to recall or connect the particulars."

Surely Beeman exaggerates. Surely there were dry eyes and unflushed cheeks aplenty in the courtroom. Still, it was by all accounts a masterful performance. A witness said Henry "was emphatic without vehemence or declamation; animated, but never boisterous; nervous, without recourse to intemperate language; and clear, though not always methodical." And from another observer: Henry "was the perfect master of the passions of his auditory, whether in the tragic or the comic line." He still might not have known the law very well, but he knew how to hold the attention of an audience and bend its opinions into the precise shape he desired. Even the judge was impressed. "Some twenty minutes earlier," writes biographer George Morgan, Henry "had been as a lout in his own father's eyes; now tears ran down his father's cheeks."

When the jurors announced their verdict this time, it was no less of a jolt than the first one had been. The Reverend James Maury, they decided, would receive his back pay all right — not in tobacco but in the coin of the realm. The amount: one penny!

The farmers erupted in cheers, some of them jumping out of their seats and pumping their arms in the air. Then they descended on the man who had so superbly represented them and lifted him onto their shoulders like the star of their team that he had proven to be. They transported him out of the courthouse and into the street, where even more grateful farmers expressed their delight — grabbing his hand, slapping him on the back, and offering their most heartfelt congratulations.

Maury remained behind, speaking to no one, sitting before the judge's bench and jurors' chairs, now empty. He had initially been taken aback by the vehemence of Henry's language: rapacious harpies, hoe-cake and milch cow and blanket snatchers. That terms like this could describe men who dedicated every hour of their lives to toiling for the Almighty offended all he held sacred and dear. And the king *a tyrant*, of all things! Maury, too, thought such sentiments treasonous, as well as sorely mistaken.

But Maury was even more taken aback by the jury's response. To be awarded a penny was to overturn the initial verdict in his favor. The reverend blamed it on that "little petty-fogging attorney" who stirred such unwarranted passions. He would soon learn something worse about Henry, and it was Henry himself who would admit it.

After the trial, Henry took Maury aside and, expecting that the preacher would bear him no grudge, confessed his insincerity. He had been more interested in making a good impression on his fellow Virginians, he told the clergyman, than in speaking the truth, more interested in achieving a measure of fame for himself than in accurately describing the natures of crown and clergy. The courtroom was a stage, Henry said, and he had not only written his part but played it to perfection.

Some historians make light of this confession. They point out that it was customary at the time for opposing counsel to meet after a trial and spend a few peaceful moments together, assuring each other that no harm was meant, that nothing personal had been intended, that they had simply been doing business as business was supposed to be done. They would shake hands, give each other a pat on the back. They were, many of them, friends outside the court-room, sometimes coworkers in various legislative matters. They wanted to keep their relationships in good repair.

But Henry and Maury were not friends, and might never have seen each other again. Maury was not Henry's opposing counsel. And Henry was not admitting to business as usual. He was bragging about how far beyond the pale he had gone, acknowledging that he had done so to serve the cause of self-aggrandizement, not justice. No relationship joined Henry and Maury, and Henry's words made certain there would never be one.

Later, Maury would write to a friend, telling him what Henry had admitted.

> After the court was adjourned, he apologized to me for what he had said, alleging that his sole view in engaging in the cause, and in saying what he had, was to render himself popular. You see, then, it is so clear a point in this person's opinion that the ready road to popularity here is to trample under the interests of reli-gion, the rights of the Church, and the prerogative of the Crown. . . . Mr. Cootes, merchant on James River, after court, said "he would have given a considerable sum out of his own pocket, rather than his friend Patrick should have been guilty of a crime . . . and justly observed that he exceeded the most seditious and inflammatory harangues of the tribunes of old Rome."

Patrick Henry's legal practice had been struggling before the Parson's Cause. Few people sought his assistance, they paid him little money, and he attracted no cases that made the populace sit up and take notice. Within a year of the Maury trial, he had 160 new clients.

He had also gained respect, becoming not only a successful attorney but one of the leading colonial spokesmen for grievances against the Crown. He was soon elected to the Virginia House of Burgesses and became one of its most influential members, his oratory there sometimes as incendiary as it had been in his father's courtroom. He attended both Continental Congresses. He served several terms as governor of Virginia, helping to recruit men for both the Continental Army and the state militia, setting up production facilities for war materiel and arranging loans to keep those facilities operating. Later, he helped draft Virginia's constitution, and later still, lobbied for adoption of the Bill of Rights to the federal constitution.

It was for Patrick Henry a long and respectable career, one largely devoted to the good of both his fellow citizens and the nation they had joined together to forge. Yet it began, less than two years before the firing of shots at Lexington and Concord, with the most shameful display of ambition by any of the Founding Fathers.

Chapter 5
Vanity

BENJAMIN FRANKLIN ADMITTED IT. Not that he was by nature a vain man, and certainly not vain to the exclusion of other qualities that people would have found more commendable. But did he enjoy being complimented from time to time, especially in the presence of others? Yes. Did he seek out praise when he thought it was deserved and could be elicited without struggle? Yes. Did he find vanity a weakness on his part or a source of offense to others? Not if he conceded it cheerfully, and he almost always did, sometimes with accompanying gestures: a smile and a shrug of the shoulders. For Franklin, it was all a matter of style.

When congratulated for the eloquence of the speech he made to bring the Constitutional Convention to a close, he wrote that the acclaim "flatters my vanity much more than a peerage could do." In this case, Franklin was confessing vanity by way of expressing gratitude. But there were occasions, he believed, when vanity could stand alone, a virtue of sorts in itself. It was an unusual position for one of the founders to take, and only Franklin could have taken it in a manner at once bold, witty, and gracious. In the first paragraph of his *Autobiography*, he writes: "Having emerg'd from the Poverty & Obscurity in which I was born & bred, to a State of Affluence & some Degree of Reputation in the World, and having gone so far thro' Life with a considerable Share of Felicity, the conducing Means I made use of, which, with the Blessing of God, so well succeeded, my Posterity may like to know, as they find some of them suitable to their own Situations, & therefore fit to be imitated."

It is a mild enough form of vanity, passing almost as self-deprecation, Franklin admitting his good fortune while attributing it to the Almighty and claiming to be relating the particulars for the good of others. That, at least, is one of the reasons. Later in the same paragraph, he goes further in defending immodesty, concluding as follows:

> And last (I may as well confess it, since my Denial of it will be believed by no body) perhaps I shall a good deal gratify my own *Vanity*. Indeed, I scarce ever heard or saw the introductory words *Without Vanity I may say,* &c but some vain thing immediately follow'd. Most people dislike Vanity in others whatever Share they have of it themselves, but I give it fair Quarter wherever I meet with it, being persuaded that it is often productive of Good to the Possessor & to others that are within his Sphere of Action: And therefore in many Cases it would not be quite absurd if a Man were to thank God for his Vanity among the other Comforts of Life.

These were not controversial passages. Most people who read the *Autobiography*, published posthumously in 1793, seemed to think that Franklin had long since earned the right to an occasional self-administered pat on the back. Besides, he wrote this portion of his book when he was sixty-five years old, an age at which men may well believe they are entitled to defend their foibles rather than apologize for them, and in some cases to insist that they are not foibles at all.

The other founders were less forgiving of vanity than Franklin. Some of them were as unwilling to own up to it as they were to ambition. To them, vanity seemed a flaunting of ambition. It was also counterproductive, for rather than advancing himself in the opinion of others, the braggart, by his very brazenness, encouraged his listeners to think less of him, thereby losing dignity in a society that placed dignity among its highest values. In most cases, to charge one with vanity was to insult him, or at least to question his character, and against no one was the charge made more often, and less fairly, than George Washington.

There was, first of all, his appearance. Washington stood six feet, two inches tall at a time when most men stood a full head shorter. He weighed 180 pounds; his waist was trim, his shoulders were broad, and his legs powerful, enabling him to sit confidently on horseback and control his mount with a minimum of effort. Dismounted, he was no less graceful, no less in control. When he stood with his aides at a military encampment, soldiers reporting for duty for the first time, although never having seen him before, could tell at once which person was their commander. Said a man who did not meet him until the last few years of the general's life, "Washington has something uncommonly majestic and commanding in his walk, his address, his figure, and his countenance." In other words, Washington did not have to utter a syllable; he *looked* like a man possessed of vanity.

Then there was his manner. Reserved and sometimes distant, he could seem annoyingly self-occupied, especially at social gatherings where others were mingling effortlessly and his grace was not apparent. But aloofness can indicate shyness as well as vanity, and shyness had its place in Washington's personality no less than courage in battle. To be aloof is also to reveal discomfort with certain kinds of conversation, settings, or company. Those who knew him best seldom found Washington aloof, and he did not leave that impression on others when the topics were familiar or meaningful to him. And no one who ever saw him at a ball, whirling around the dance floor, as he had been doing since he started taking lessons at the age of fifteen, could possibly have thought him remote or self-absorbed.

There was also his eminence. He had been a skilled surveyor as a young man and the successful owner and manager of a large, well-run estate after that. He had fought cunningly, if not always effectively, in the French and Indian War. He had served as the first commander in chief of the Continental Army in the Revolutionary War, the most powerful position in the colonies at the time. He had been the most important man to attend the Constitutional Convention, not because he was its president but because even though his direct contributions to the document were minimal, he inspired in those who wrote the Constitution a desire to win his approbation with their efforts. And, of course, he went on to become the first president of the United States, setting precedents for behavior in office that still exist today. In the eyes of some, a man with credentials like this could not help but be vain, regardless of his true nature.

Finally there was his plumage. As head of the colonial fighting forces, Washington was meticulous about attire, designing uniforms for his men and insisting on fabrics of the highest quality for himself. "Mr. Parish is at work to make you the best Hatt in his power," his deputy quartermaster general wrote to him in 1779. In 1782, Washington asked for "the neatest and best Leather Breeches" available, perhaps of "a skin called I think, the Carrabous, of which very neat Breeches were made." And the following year he found himself "in want of as much superfine Buff cloth (not of the yellow kind) as would make a Vest Coat Breeches."

To his first inaugural ball Washington wore a brown silk suit, uncommonly dapper garb for the time and tailored precisely to his proportions. Once he began working daily in the President's House, he asked for "as much superfine blk broad Cloth" as possible for his office wardrobe, having his secretary specify that it be "the best superfine French or Dutch black, exceedingly fine, of a soft silky texture, not glossy like the Engh. Clothes." Then for his second inauguration he wore a black velvet suit, the front pockets of which were lined with linen and two other pockets with a velvet facing.

In part, Washington dressed as he did as commander in chief and chief executive to show his respect for the offices, and to try to encourage that respect in others. But he had been preoccupied with his dress from his first days as a surveyor. Such a concern for appearances is a form of vanity, but a benign one, and as far as onlookers are concerned, much preferable to its opposite — a complete disregard for appearance and the impression it makes on others.

It was inevitable, though, that for this reason if no other, newspapers opposing Washington would accuse him of conceit, and claim that he demonstrated it on a variety of occasions: by a brusque manner to subordinates, by an elevated nose and disdainful expression at government functions, and by "stately journeying through the American continent in search of personal incense."

Actually, there were times when Washington confessed to a certain degree of self-satisfaction, but in the humblest of manners. In 1782, learning that certain French military and judicial officers had expressed their admiration for his conduct of the Revolutionary War, he had to admit that while it was "highly flattering to my vanity, at the same time it has a first claim to all my gratitude."

But like Franklin reacting to the accolades for his address at the Constitutional Convention, what Washington was really doing here was stating his appreciation for the regard of others, not admitting to a high opinion of himself. Washington's true attitude toward vanity was probably demonstrated most clearly when the poet Phillis Wheatley sent him her ode in the early days of the war. The general responded promptly, expressing his appreciation and then turning the praise back on her. "I thank you most sincerely," he wrote, "for your polite notice of me, in the elegant Lines you enclosed, and however undeserving I may be of such encomium and panegyrick, the style and manner exhibit a striking proof of your great poetical talents."

Then, and most revealingly, he continued. "I would have published the Poem, had I not been apprehensive that, while I only
meant to give the World this new instance of your genius, I might
have incurred the imputation of Vanity. This and nothing else, determined me not to give it place in the public Prints."

Jefferson and Hamilton would not want to incur such an imputation
either, although the former was the less likely candidate.

Jefferson was a man comfortable "in the bosom of my family," a
man who found stimulation in "my farm, my books, and my neigh-
bors." A vain man usually prefers a bigger audience. When he left
Monticello in 1797, heading north to be sworn in as vice president
to Adams to Philadelphia, he wrote to James Madison: "I shall escape
into the city as covertly as possible. If [Pennsylvania] Governor Mif-
flin should show any symptoms of ceremony, pray contrive to parry
them." A vain man prefers pomp to anonymity.

Jefferson was not totally free from immodesty. No man of his
abilities could be. He believed, for instance, that the desk upon which
he had written the Declaration of Independence should be considered a national treasure and would increase in value with the passing
years. "Politics, as well as religion, has its superstitions," he explained.
"These gaining strength with time may one day give imaginary value
to this relic, for its associations with the birth of the Great Charter of
our Independence."

But such comments were rare for Jefferson. In fact, one of the
few direct references he ever made to vanity was to deny being
afflicted with it. During the war, after he had slunk back to Monticello following his less than glorious tenure as Virginia's governor, he
learned that the colony's assembly had passed a resolution calling for
a panel to investigate his behavior in office. Jefferson was to be
probed, prodded, and perhaps condemned. His enemies, it seemed,
were trying to turn the entire assembly against him.

But they couldn't. The effort stalled. Jefferson's foes either lost
heart, decided they had gone too far, or didn't have enough support

for their campaign and turned to other matters. Whatever the case, the panel never formed, and Jefferson — officially, if not socially — was exonerated.

But he had long since exonerated himself. He thought he had done the best he could as the colony's governor under difficult circumstances and fumed that the legislature would even consider an official inquiry, so much so that he made a vow he would break more than once in the years ahead: he determined never to subject himself to government employment again.

In the spring of 1782, however, Madison wrote to suggest just such a thing, though not specifying the office Jefferson might hold. Jefferson took his time in replying, and when he did it was in steps. First, he said, he "examined well my heart to know whether it were thoroughly cured of every principle of political ambition." He concluded that it was. Then he declared that "every individual if called on to an equal tour of political duty" must accept that duty, "yet it can never go so far as to submit to it his whole existence." Finally, making a connection between "public service & private misery," he told Madison, "I have not the vanity to count myself among those whom the state would think worth oppressing with perpetual service."

Much oppression, of course, lay ahead for Jefferson, both in the United States and abroad, and he had just enough vanity to expect, and welcome, his nation's call.

That same year, Hamilton also had much service ahead of him — political, military, and journalistic. He would not refer to it as oppression, however, not even in jest. Positions of influence were to him a series of opportunities for Ciceronian fame, and, with the exception of Washington, he could think of no one more deserving than himself. He was proud of the distance he had traveled, socially more than geographically, since his fatherless childhood in the Caribbean. No sooner had he arrived in America in 1772 than he found a number of highly placed men who realized his potential and were eager to help him achieve it. Some treated him as a surrogate son, some as a protégé. Others allowed him to assist them in their businesses — and all found him so capable in his roles that they eventually steered him to Washington. The more time he spent in the company of his bene-factors, the more pleased with himself he became.

He was also pleased with his accomplishments since 1772, not only the tasks he performed during the war and his election to Con-gress afterward but also a series of pamphlets he had written before the war even began, advocating independence from Great Britain. Was he too pleased? Some thought so, and not just those who object-ed to the brand of big-government Federalism he came to espouse. Gouverneur Morris, who considered himself a friend, found Hamil-ton "indiscreet, vain, and opinionated." George Cabot, less a friend than an acquaintance, thought Hamilton showed too much "egotism and vanity." And later, when Hamilton wrote a pamphlet called *Let-ter from Alexander Hamilton, Concerning the Public Conduct and Charac-ter of John Adams, Esq. President of the United States*, which was highly critical of Adams for both his conduct *and* his character, Abigail Adams blasted the author for his "weakness, vanity, and ambitious views." Vanity, Abigail thought, because Hamilton believed he should be president rather than her husband, and his ego could not accept the fact that his foreign birth disqualified him.

To be fair, Adams's previous disregard for Hamilton had inspired the pamphlet. When Hamilton was secretary of the treasury under Washington, Adams found much to dislike in his policies, especially Hamilton's proposed reforms of banking and finance, including both import tariffs and excise taxes. Adams objected not only to the meas-ures, but to the secretary's cocksureness that they were the wisest of all possible courses the nation could take, so wise that Hamilton would not deign to modify them or even debate them with others. Vanity was proof of "littleness of mind," Adams once said, and by this definition Hamilton's mind was far too tiny for the tasks it pursued.

On one occasion, Adams complained to Jefferson about Hamil-ton, and Adams couldn't have found a better audience. Defamation of Hamilton was a favorite topic for Jefferson, and he delighted in Adams's dismissal of him as an "insolent coxcomb who rarely dined in good company where there was good wine without getting silly and vaporing about his administration, like a young girl about her brilliants and trinkets."

At a later time, Adams claimed that Hamilton "had been blown up with vanity by the Tories." He might have had a point. Hamilton had a habit of inflating when he got his way, of referring to himself a little too much and seeming to strut when he should have been placing one foot before the other in conventional fashion — and in Washington's first administration he got his way more often than not.

But to some extent Hamilton's vanity was in the eye of the beholder, especially the hostile beholder. Certainly there was another side to him, a side that demonstrated concern for others more than an exaggerated regard for himself. Hamilton seldom refused a friend who asked for a loan, and when a painter whom he especially admired fell on hard times and was shipped off to debtors' prison, Hamilton sent his wife to the prison to sit for him. Eliza Hamilton, in turn, persuaded other women to slip behind bars and sit for their portraits, and those women persuaded others — until finally the prison was admitting so many gentle-ladies that it had become a women's tea society as much as a place of incarceration for debtors. The painter, Ralph Earl, accumulated enough money from all the commissions to pay off his debts and regain his freedom.

Hamilton helped another friend secure employment, recommending his barber to Tobias Lear, Washington's presidential secretary. "I have found him sober and punctual & he has done my business to my satisfaction," Hamilton wrote. "He desires to have the honor of dealing with the heads and chins of some of your family and I give him this line, at his request, to make him known to you."

And Hamilton was capable of kindnesses of a more tender sort. "One evening when Hamilton and other New York lawyers were riding the circuit along with Judge James Kent, Kent retired early, feeling ill. Later that night, Kent overheard Hamilton come into his room to put an extra blanket on him: 'Sleep warm, little judge, and get well. What should we do if anything should happen to you?' "

Was Adams also guilty of "littleness of mind"? He, too, was denounced as vain, perhaps more often than Hamilton, and he did not take it well. In 1781, he had been assigned to the Netherlands to secure both recognition of and financial assistance for the soon-to-be United States. As ever, he was devoting long hours and great concentration to his tasks and was, as ever, feeling grossly underappreciated. He was about to feel it even more. Robert Livingston, recently appointed foreign secretary, the first man to hold that position in America, wrote Adams a letter accusing him of not keeping Congress informed of his activities. Furthermore, Livingston said, he had learned that Adams made "a ridiculous display" before the Dutch Court and, in short, that he was much too concerned with self-puffery to be representing his homeland in a proper manner.

The charge was ridiculous. Adams had secured a loan of two million dollars from the Dutch, less than Congress had hoped for but more than Adams and other realists had thought possible. In addition, he had arranged the loan at the favorable rate of five percent. "I know the unflinching character of Mr. Adams," wrote Baron Joan Derk van der Capellen tot den Pol, with whom Adams had been working on the loan, and other Dutch negotiators knew his character, too. All of them admired him.

Adams erupted when he read Livingston's letter. "The charge of vanity is the last resort of little wits and mercenary quacks, the vainest men alive, against me and measures that they can find no other objection to." Adams would not stand for Livingston's accusations, of vanity or anything else. "I have long since learned that a man may give offense and yet succeed." And he believed that, at this mission, he was succeeding admirably.

But Livingston was not the only person who charged Adams with vanity, and others could make a better case. They could tell of times when Adams not only boasted about his accomplishments but embellished them, and times when he either conversed snippily or refused to converse at all with a person he thought beneath him. When he learned that Adams was about to depart from the Netherlands to rejoin Franklin and John Jay in Paris, Jefferson wrote to Madison in language so incendiary that he sent the letter in code. Adams, Jefferson said, "hates Franklin, he hates Jay, he hates the French, he hates the English. To whom will he adhere? His vanity is a lineament in his character which had entirely escaped me."

It had not escaped some of his detractors in Congress, however. When Adams became Washington's vice president, they "honored" him in verse.

> I'll tell in a trice —
> 'Tis old Daddy Vice
> Who carries of pride an ass-load;
> Who turns up his nose
> Wherever he goes,
> With vanity swelled like a toad.

As was the case with Hamilton, though, the preceding tells only part of the story. Adams was a brilliant, courageous, sensitive man. Perhaps too brilliant; he had little patience at times for those of lesser intellect. Perhaps too courageous; he could be uncompromising when compromise was the only practical solution to a problem. Perhaps too sensitive; he felt the sting of rejection when none was intended. He was guilty of the last of these during one of his many separations from Abigail. Accused of braggadocio, Adams picked up his pen and explained that he could not be guilty of such a thing because its repercussions were too heinous. "Whenever Vanity, and Gaiety, a Love of Pomp and Dress . . . get the better of the Principles and Judgments of Men or Women there is no knowing where they will stop, nor into what Evils, natural, moral, or political, they will lead us."

For reasons like this, Adams swore he would not write an auto-biography. "As the Lives of Physlosophers, Statesmen or Historians written by them selves have generally been suspected of Vanity," he once stated, "and therefore few people have been able to read them without disgust, there is no reason to expect that any Sketches I may leave of my own Times would be received by the Public with any favour, or read by individuals with much interest."

Then, later, specifically about himself, all vanity cast aside for the moment: "My Life has been too trifling and my Actions too insignificant for me to write for the Public to read."

Of course he changed his mind. Of course he wrote an autobi-ography. In fact, he wrote one much longer and more detailed than Franklin's, thinking it a valuable record of important times, a unique perspective on momentous events, a guidebook for future genera-tions. Adams also knew that to write the story of one's life is to con-fess to a certain conceit, and his was great enough that he couldn't always protest his innocence. "Vanity, I am sensible," he wrote to a friend in 1801, "is my cardinal vice and cardinal folly, and I am in continual Danger, when in Company, of being led an ignis fatuus* Chase by it, without the strictest Caution and watchfulness over my self."

There was, not just for John Adams but for all the founders, only one cure for vanity, and it was not unanimously practiced.

---

*A flashing light seen over marshes, supposedly caused by the spontaneous com-bustion of gases. Figuratively, something illusory or misleading. (Literally "foolish fire.")

Chapter 6
Modesty

IN 1771, ADAMS WAS ELECTED to the colonial legislature, his first public office but one that offered no remuneration. As soon as the votes had been tallied the questions arose, persistent and demanding. What had he gotten himself into? He was already overworked at his legal practice. Where would he find the time for legislative duties? He was already underpaid at his legal practice. Where would he find the money to replace the income he would now begin to lose? And his wife was about to give birth to their third child. How would he find the time *and* money to support his family?

Adams felt the pressure like a physical weight or a knife wound. He suffered panic attacks, sudden and overwhelming feelings of dread — unforeseen and uncontrollable. One night, a few months before going off to the legislature, he went out to dinner with friends and associates, expecting a pleasant evening. Yet, as he wrote in his diary, he "came home in great Anxiety and distress, and had a most unhappy Night — never in more misery, in my whole Life — God grant, I may never see such another Night."

He was to see many others. Not long after the legislative session began, he suffered another panic attack that left him emotionally paralyzed for several days. This time he understood the reason, or thought he did. It was not just that he was toiling longer than before, not just that he was receiving so little pay, not just that his country-men were beginning to talk about war — it was all the speaking he had to do before his fellow legislators and other local assemblies. He wasn't used to being so public a figure. He might still have admired Cicero, but was certainly not in the great Roman's class as an orator. The strains of addressing his fellow lawmakers "had exhausted my health, brought on pain in my breast and complaint in my lungs, which seriously threatened my life," he later said. He hadn't realized the demands that fame made on those who chased it.

And the pressure only mounted. There was no end in sight, and at times he could not even imagine one. "What an Atom," he said of himself on a night of special blackness, and then went on to refer to himself as nothing more than an "Animalcule," an organism that can be seen only under a microscope.

Such modesty — self-abnegation, even — was not typical of Adams, even in his early years. But to be understood accurately, it needs to be seen in a context both larger and simpler than the one in which it occurred. Adams's comment falls into one of several con-flicting sets of traits that make up the personalities of all human beings: strength and weakness, enthusiasm and lassitude, sensitivity and hardheadedness, generosity and hard-heartedness, hope and despair. And vanity and modesty.

Usually, when Adams broke into a few bars of a humble tune, it was not to pity himself, but to deny the opposing sentiment: that he had developed too high an opinion of himself. In his autobiography he told of "a great Truth of which I have had abundant Experience . . . that He who builds on Popularity is like a Sailor on a topmast whether drunk or sober, ready at the first blast to plunge into the briny deep." And to his wife, in the momentous summer of 1776, his earlier troubles behind him and his confidence rebuilding, he wrote, "A Man must be selfish, even to acquire great Popularity. He must grasp for himself, under specious Pretences, for the public Good, and he must attach himself to his Relations, Connections and Friends, by becoming a Champion for their Interests, in order to form a Phalanx about him . . . to make them Trumpeters of his Praise, and sticklers for his Fame, Fortune, and Honour." It was not the kind of behavior, Adams implied, in which he would not indulge — although it was precisely the kind in which he did.

Yet it was an odd time for him to make such a statement. The preceding month Adams had served on the drafting committee for the Declaration of Independence and had done so, according to Jefferson, illustriously: "No man better merited than Mr. John Adams to hold a most conspicuous place in the design. He was the pillar of its support on the floor of Congress, its ablest advocate and defender against the multifarious assaults encountered."

Because of the Declaration, the summer of 1776 ranked as the starting point of Adams's true renown. Still, he did not quite believe it, could not really accept it. He felt compelled to make his infrequent bows toward humility, as if Abigail were whispering in his ear, reminding him of his manners. Or as if a clergyman were whispering into his other ear, cautioning him that pride goeth before a fall. One day he would write about "Men of extraordinary Fame, to which I have no Pretensions," but by then, having served as the second president of the United States, he had become one of those men. It was, of course, where his pretensions had been steering him all along.

Sometimes when Adams was feeling modest, or feeling that he *should* be feeling modest, he and Abigail would trade metaphors on the subject, a little game they played a few times, the administering of a placebo to John's ego. "Let the Butterflies of Fame glitter with their Wings," Adams once wrote to his wife. "I shall envy neither their Musick nor their Colours." And she to him when the subject came up again a few years later: "I know the voice of Fame to be a mere weathercock, unstable as Water and fleeting as a Shadow." It was her way of cheering her husband on those occasions when she was not cheering him with assurances that his own fame would be as stable and permanent as a mountain range.

For Franklin, modesty was less a matter of substance than a branch of etiquette, something in which a person indulged not so much out of sincerity as out of consideration for others. It was small talk, and when someone made small talk he did not hesitate to mention his shortcomings, offhanded references with no particular heft, as likely as not to be forgotten by those listening. In other situations, when someone conversed about the important issues of the day, he spoke with candor and assertiveness. If others thought him vain as a result, so be it.

An inveterate list maker, Franklin once decided on virtue as a heading and jotted down all the virtues he could think of. It took him only a few minutes, and he did not include modesty. He added it later not because he regretted the omission, but because a friend complained that the list was incomplete without it. Rather than argue, Franklin attached the trait to the end of his list, perhaps thinking that by adding it he was practicing it.

His first significant contribution to American journalism was a series of letters he wrote to the *New England Courant*, a newspaper run by his older brother James. The year was 1722, Benjamin a mere sixteen years old. Afraid that James would not publish the letters if he knew they had been written by his younger brother — a mere apprentice in the *Courant's* print shop and a constant source of chagrin to his sibling — Benjamin took the name Silence Dogood, a sixty-year-old widow who "lived a cheerful country life." He began the first of the articles boldly, announcing that, as the widow Dogood, he intended to write a column of sorts for the *Courant's* readers once every two weeks, "which I presume will add somewhat to their entertainment." Mrs. Dogood concluded: "I am not insensible of the impossibility of pleasing all, but I would not willingly displease any."

In other words: the show of self-confidence was the lead, humility the afterthought. In conventional journalistic fashion, Franklin put the most important clues to his personality first, then gradually worked his way down to the less essential. Whether writing as himself or under some other nom de plume, Franklin was simply too ebullient a person to do anything more than pay lip service to modesty.

Hamilton's feelings were similar. He did not mean to offend others with displays of vanity, but a man with deeply held convictions cannot help but seem overbearing. If modesty tempered those convictions, admitting the possibility of error, Hamilton simply could not partake of it. Dishonesty to one's self, Hamilton believed, was a greater flaw than immodesty.

In truth, Hamilton might best be thought of as a-modest. The quality neither applied to him nor interested him. He would not have found a place for it had he compiled his own list of virtues — or vices, for that matter. He believed that he dedicated his life to ideas that were intended for the betterment of society as a whole. What, he might conceivably have asked, could be a greater show of humility than that?

One of his friends, Tench Tilghman, served as Hamiton's "faithful assistant" for five years during the Revolutionary War. In that time, Tilghman saw Hamilton at his best and worst. He saw Hamilton in cold, hunger, penury, and military defeat. He saw Hamilton succeed in battle but face rejection time after time when he pleaded for further commands. Through it all, Tilghman found Hamilton a man of "modesty and love of concord." Had the war continued, Tilghman implied, he would willingly have spent another five years with him.

★   ★   ★

Jefferson was a different sort altogether, always a different sort from Hamilton. A reticent man tends toward modesty, regardless of his achievements and his own opinion of them, because it suits his temperament. A bookish man tends toward modesty, regardless of the knowledge he acquires, because he stands in awe of the knowledge of those from whom he has learned. A poor public speaker tends toward modesty, regardless of his eloquence on the page, because he fears that others will find him wanting as a performer. Jefferson was all three.

In 1784, Jefferson joined Franklin and John Adams in France to negotiate various trade pacts for the United States, and Congress intended to have him take over for Franklin after a few months. Jefferson, however, did not think such a thing truly possible. "Is it you, sir," a Frenchman supposedly asked him, "who will replace Franklin?" "No sir, I succeed him," he replied. "No one can replace him."

In fact, as Joseph J. Ellis points out, modesty was not just an ingredient of Jefferson's personality but an element of his philosophy of government, which clarified itself when he assumed the presidency. "Political power," Ellis writes, "to fit the republican model, needed to be exercised unobtrusively, needed neither to feel or to look like power at all." Ellis goes on to describe Jefferson's "self-consciously unimperial executive style. . . . When Jefferson prepared his first Annual Message to Congress, for example, all the department heads were asked to submit memoranda suggesting items for inclusion." He would not run roughshod over the opinions of others, nor insist on the supremacy of his own without allowing them to be challenged.

Jefferson's vanity ran deep but was not often discernible. His modesty appeared on the surface, not because it was a disguise or a facade, but just the opposite. It was his natural manner, and revealed itself for all to see.

Surprisingly enough, Patrick Henry had grown modest as well — or at least less concerned with the opinions of others. His rhetoric still sizzled, but, with the Parson's Cause behind him now, it was the struggle for American independence, rather than the struggle to make a name for himself, that fired his eloquence. Two years after the Maury trial, he addressed the Virginia House of Burgesses on the Stamp Act. "Caesar had his Brutus," he declared, "Charles the First his Cromwell; and George the Third — *may profit by their example. If this be treason, make the most of it.*"

And a month before the Revolutionary War began, Henry spoke in equally incendiary terms to the Virginia Convention:

> The gentlemen may cry, Peace, peace! but there is no peace. The war has actually begun! The next gale that sweeps from the north will bring to our ears the clash of resounding arms! Our brethren are already in the field! Why stand we here idle? What is it that the gentlemen wish? What would they have? Is life so dear or peace so sweet as to be purchased at the price of chains and slavery? Forbid it, Almighty God. I know not what course others may take, but as for me, give me liberty or give me death!

This ranks among the most famous excerpts of all colonial discourse, and many of the other founders did what they could to publicize it. Henry did nothing. He did not publish his speeches in newspapers or hand out copies to friends or even try to increase the size of his audience by announcing in advance that he would be giving an especially eloquent address on a given day. In fact, some people believe that Henry memorized his speeches before presenting them, then ripped them up and threw them away, preferring to seem spontaneous rather than to be seen reciting. Historians can quote a few of his speeches today with some confidence because listeners made transcriptions either as Henry spoke or moments afterward. His reputation was such that, when he opened his mouth in formal venues, paper was immediately produced and pens dipped into inkwells.

Henry showed a similar modesty as a legislator and administrator, writing resolutions, advocating laws, and trying to do what he thought best for his colony, then all the colonies, and then the nation that the colonies became — but he made no demands for public recognition when he succeeded — or, as he would have put it, when the *measures* succeeded. He didn't keep his notes, nor, as was common at the time, did he write up and print his own version of events.

James Maury would have been stunned at the transformation. It was as if Henry had come to think of fame as a club, and once you were admitted, you were a member for life. No longer did he have to submit to the baser forms of ambition and self-aggrandizement and other rituals of initiation. No longer did he have to accuse clergymen of stealing hoe-cakes and denying milk to widows and orphans. Instead, he could simply do his work, confident that the work would matter to the future of his country.

And of course, some people are modest for other reasons — not because they believe it a social grace or a means of counterbalancing vanity or a sign that they have been accepted into the club. They are modest because they doubt themselves. Not at all times, not on all occasions, but they wonder whether they are qualified for at least some of their responsibilities. They question their background, their education, the verdict of posterity on their actions. George Washington, a man eulogized as "first in war, first in peace, and first in the hearts of his countrymen," known for having earned a place in the hearts of men in other countries, a symbol of the war for independence and the beginnings of nationhood more than anyone of his generation — George Washington, who would not publish Phillis Wheatley's poem for fear of the imputation of vanity, was in many ways a modest man.

His early days as a soldier gave him reason. His first command in the French and Indian War resulted in the surrender of Fort Necessity, a redoubt that he and his troops had built in 1754 in western Pennsylvania but had not been able to defend. When the enemy attacked, there were 400 men inside the fort, many of them sick and all of them underfed. Their attempts to hold their position lasted a single day. The French and Indians began firing on the morning of

BENJAMIN FRANKLIN
(1706–1790)
Ambassador, author, inventor, scientist, and America's first true celebrity
Engraving by H. B. Hall after the painting by J. A. Duplessis (1783)
courtesy Library of Congress

SAMUEL ADAMS
(1722–1803)
Mendacious journalist
and firebrand
by John Singleton Copley
(1772)
courtesy HumanitiesWeb.org

BUTTON GWINNETT
(1732–1777)
The first signer of
the Declaration
of Independence
to die violently
courtesy Library of Congress

GEORGE WASHINGTON
(1732–1799)
Father of the country,
accomplished dancer,
and painstaking
clothing designer
by Gilbert Stuart (1796)
courtesy the Yorck Project

JOHN ADAMS
(1735–1826)
Expert lawyer, meticulous
diplomat, and frustrated
seeker of fame
by Charles Wilson Peale (1791)
courtesy Teaching Politics

PATRICK HENRY
(1736–1799)
One-time questionable lawyer and incendiary orator
by George Bagby Matthews (1891)
courtesy Senate.gov

JOHN HANCOCK

(1737–1793)

Famous for his extra-legible signature on the Declaration and infamous for holding a British customs officer captive to avoid paying taxes on a shipful of wine

by John Singleton Copley
(c. 1770–7?)

courtesy Teaching Politics

JAMES WILSON

(1742–1798)

The only person ever to be a member of the Supreme Court and a fugitive from the law at the same time

courtesy University of St. Andrews

THOMAS JEFFERSON
(1743–1826)
Beleaguered governor of Virginia and the most famous founder
not to know what to make of his fame

courtesy WhiteHouse.gov

BENJAMIN RUSH
(1745–1813)
Surgeon general to the
Continental Army and the
father of American psychiatry
by Charles Wilson Peale (1783)
courtesy Wikimedia Commons

JAMES MADISON
(1751–1836)
Notoriously taciturn
Engraved by Pendleton's
Lithography after the painting
by Gilbert Stuart (1828)
courtesy Library of Congress

GOUVERNEUR MORRIS

(1752–1816)
Head of the committee
responsible for the final draft
of the Constitution
Engraved after a drawing by Pierre
Eugène Du Simitière (1783)
courtesy Library of Congress

ALEXANDER HAMILTON

(1755–1804)
Washington's right hand,
first secretary of the treasury,
and ill-fated duelist
by John Trumbull (1792)
courtesy Wikimedia Commons

July 3 and did not stop until Washington capitulated, a quarter of his troops dead or wounded, at midnight.

In a later battle, this time as an aide to British general Edward Braddock and still feeling the effects of a monthlong fever, Washington had his horse shot out from under him, a disgrace for a soldier. He replaced the horse with another, and *that* one was shot out from under him, too — a doubly embarrassing turn, setting new standards either of ineptitude or bad luck. His temperature surely rose another degree or two.

Events didn't go much better for his cohorts. The French and Indians routed the much larger British-American force in a surprise attack, and Braddock was killed. If Washington received any credit for his role in the engagement, it was merely for surviving. Most of his fellow soldiers were either dead, dying, or badly injured.

Shortly afterward, Washington was released from military service. He believed himself to have been dismissed for incompetence, although this does not seem to have been the case. Nonetheless, he rode forlornly back to Mount Vernon, later writing to his brother that his career as a soldier had been the worst experience of his life. He had lost his health, served with men who were themselves unhealthy as well as poorly trained, received payment for little more than expenses, and met one defeat after another. He did not have much of a future, he told his brother, in the military.

He received a summons and returned to the battlefield shortly afterward but didn't fare much better this time. Perhaps the most important lesson Washington learned from the French and Indian War — one that sustained him through the bleak early days of the next war he fought — was that the British army consisted of men far less skilled and courageous than he had previously believed. Given the right circumstances, and a strong enough sense of commitment, it could be beaten — and not just by an alliance of Europeans and natives.

That next war stood twenty years away, and when it came, Washington still doubted his aptitude for the soldier's life. The

Second Continental Congress, however, had no such reservations. Or no better choices. They decided on Washington to head the colonial fighting forces in the war against the Crown, and believed he would fill the position admirably. Washington had, after all, been one of the highest-ranking American officers in the French and Indian War, and despite his failures, the war had ended in something of a draw. Actually, it had not so much ended as begun a lengthy process of trickling out, with the French withdrawing their troops from North America and various Indian tribes, especially the Ottawa under Chief Pontiac, continuing randomly to attack colonial settlements in out of the way locations with unpredictable brutality.

The night that Washington was named commander in chief, some of the delegates to the Continental Congress took him out to dinner. Spirits ran high at the meal, the men eating steaks, drinking heartily, and toasting the success of their new leader. They called for a speech. Washington responded as confidently as he could. The next morning, he addressed the Congress at the State House in Philadelphia: "Mr. President, Tho' I am truly sensible of the high Honour done me in this Appointment, yet I feel great distress, from a consciousness that my abilities & Military experience may not be equal to the extensive & important Trust: However, as the Congress desire it, I will enter upon the momentous duty, & exert every power I Possess In their service & for the Support of the glorious Cause. I beg they will accept my most cordial thanks for this distinguished testimony of their Approbation."

The Second Continental Congress happily accepted his gratitude, but Washington continued to feel great distress. More than any other American, he now held the future of the colonies in his hands, and he doubted whether he could meet the challenge. After another three days, he wrote to his brother-in-law Burwell Bassett.

> I am now Imbarked on a tempestuous Ocean from whence, perhaps, no friendly harbour is to be found. . . . It is an honour I by no means aspired to — It is an honour I wished to avoid, as well

from an unwilling-ness to quit the peaceful enjoyment of my Family as from a thorough conviction of my own Incapacity & want of experience in the conduct of so momentous a concern — but the partiality of Congress added to some political motives, left me without a choice — May God grant therefore that my acceptance of it may be attended with some good to the common cause & without Injury (from want of knowledge) to my own reputation — I can answer but for three things, a firm belief of the justice of our Cause — close attention in the prosecution of it — and the strictest Integrety — If these cannot supply the places of Ability & Experience, the cause will suffer, & more than probable my character along with it, as reputation derives its principal support from success — but it will be remembered I hope that no desire, or insinuation of mine, placed me in this situation.

It is a revealing passage, as Washington confesses both his feelings of inadequacy and his ongoing concern for the regard of others. Never before had the two been so closely linked for him in so important a quest.

Because the war began poorly for the Americans, Washington's modesty sank to levels approaching depression. Early in 1776, after the British won the battle of Bunker Hill, burned what is now Portland, Maine, and defeated the American troops led by then loyal Benedict Arnold in the battle of Quebec, Washington reached a nadir. He did not give up or shirk his duties. He continued to command his men and strove for victory with all possible effort. Inwardly, though, doubt spread through him like a virus. He felt every bit the animalcule that Adams once had.

One day, in a moment of weakness, he confessed to his adjutant general Joseph Reed,

I have often thought how much happier I should have been if, instead of accepting a command under such circumstances, I had

taken my musket upon my shoulders and entered the ranks, or, if
I could have justified the measure to posterity and my own conscience, had retired to the back country, and lived in a wigwam
— If I shall be able to rise superior to these, and many other difficulties, which might be innumerated, I shall most religiously
believe that the finger of Providence is in it, to blind the Eyes of
our Enemys; for surely if we get well throw this Month, it must
be for want of their knowing the disadvantages we labour under.

Washington could never have imagined that four years later
Reed and his wife would name their child after him.

Eventually, Washington took up residence not in a wigwam or on
the frontier but in the President's House in Philadelphia. After the
colonists had defeated Cornwallis at Yorktown, Virginia — the war's
unofficial end — Americans were looking ahead. They were thinking about the nation they would form, the shape it would take, and
the type of ruler who should preside over it. Some people, still
believing that the British example was worth following, that the
problem had not been the throne but its particular occupant, wanted that ruler to have kingly powers.

Washington disagreed. Already suspecting that he would be the
first man to head the new country, he cautioned against granting the
nation's new leader excessive powers. "Let me conjure you then," he
informed a correspondent, "if you have any respect for your Country, concern for yourself or posterity, or respect for me, to banish
these thoughts from your Mind, and never communicate, as from
yourself, or anyone else, sentiments of a like nature."

Washington claimed that he did not want to be the leader of
the United States. Writing to his friend, the Marquis de Lafayette,
who had raised the subject of the presidency in a previous letter,
Washington said that he was now enjoying his days at Mount Vernon, "under the shadow of my own Vine and my own Fig-tree, free

from the bustle of a camp and the busy scenes of public life." It was the perfect place, he continued, to solace himself "with those tranquil enjoyments, of which the Soldier who is ever in pursuit of fame, the Statesman whose watchful days and sleepless nights are spent in devising schemes to promote the welfare of his own, perhaps the ruin of other countries . . . can have very little conception."

Three months later, Lafayette brought up the presidency again. Washington repeated his yearnings to remain where he was, telling Lafayette that "the increasing infirmities of nature and the growing love of retirement do not permit me to entertain a wish beyond that of living and dying an honest man on my own farm. Let those follow the pursuits of ambition and fame, who have a keener relish for them, or who may have more years, in store, for the enjoyment." He was not being coy or disingenuous, simply telling his good friend in Paris that he doubted his suitability for so prominent a role as the first president of the United States.

In March of the following year, by the virtually unanimous consent of his countrymen, the prominent role was his

With few exceptions, American newspapers were pleased with the choice of Washington to head their government, treating him in their columns like the monarch he didn't want to be. He wished they would restrain their language. Better yet, he wished they would write about something else. He believed that "the extravagant (and I may say undue) praises which they are heaping upon me at this moment" would eventually become "equally extravagant (that I will fondly hope unmerited) censures."

In the spring of 1791, when Washington was making the tour of the southern states that would allow Hamilton, Jefferson, and Adams to dine together and discuss their differing visions of ambition, the president was greeted warmly at every stop. To the citizens of Charleston, South Carolina, he sent a letter of appreciation.

Gentlemen,

The gratification you are pleased to express, at my arrival in your metropolis, is replied to with sincerity, in a grateful acknowledgement of the pleasing sensations which your affectionate urbanity has excited — Highly sensible of your attachment and favorable opinions, I entreat you to be persuaded of the lasting gratitude which they impress, and of the cordial regard with which they are returned.

A few weeks later, he was equally moved by his reception in Salisbury, North Carolina, where the "expressions of satisfaction on my arrival . . . are received with pleasure, and thanked with sincerity." He continued: "The interest, which you are pleased to take in my personal welfare, excites a sensibility proportioned to your goodness."

Washington wrote these and similar letters himself. He had no press secretary to ghostwrite his thank-you notes or suggest they be written in the first place. He had no campaign consultant to point out that gratitude now would win votes in the next election. These sentiments were Washington's alone, as was the urge to share them with the appropriate parties. The modest man considers the feelings of others and the contributions he can make to their well-being, especially when they have demonstrated that *his* well-being matters so much to them.

Chapter 7
Jealousy

FAME IS LIKE CAPITALISM. Each, as an ideal, is a system of opportunities and rewards, the latter going to those who best respond to the former. But neither exists as an ideal, ever has, or ever will. Skill can show itself in a variety of ways. What seems like dedication to one person can look like ambition run amok to another, and results are subject to different interpretations by different people. It is inevitable that those who don't believe they have received their just rewards will be jealous of those whose rewards they find excessive — whether in the form of remuneration or renown.

Yet among the founders, with but a single exception, little jealousy appears. Perhaps they were so satisfied with their own triumphs that they saw no reason to envy others. Perhaps they were too noble for such pettiness. Or perhaps they dared not reveal an ignoble side, seldom admitting it to themselves, and leaving behind no incriminating details for those who would later write their stories.

You can, of course, find animosity, and Jefferson and Hamilton provide the best example. They were united in the cause of inde pendence, both patriots of unquestioned commitment, but once the Revolutionary War ended, so did their amity. They morphed into antagonists from their first exchange of postwar views, when Hamilton showed himself to be a Federalist, believing power should reside in a large, centralized government, while Jefferson became the chief republican spokesman, wanting the states to maintain, if not increase, their powers. To Hamilton, the proper symbol of the new nation was the financier, merchant, or trader; to Jefferson, the farmer. Hamilton envisioned the future; Jefferson sought to extend the past.

Both men were famous at the time of their disputes and, as a result their views were publicized more widely and taken more seriously than they would have been otherwise. But it was differing positions on the questions of the day that led to their mutual antagonism, not fits of envy. Neither longed for anything tangible or ideological that the other possessed. In fact, to the extent that any of the Founding Fathers were competitors — and all of them were — it was their visions of the American future for which they competed, not the dissemination of their names. With, of course, that one exception.

It was not Benjamin Franklin. As far as anyone knows, Franklin was never jealous of anyone. On one occasion he did claim that others were jealous of him, especially when he first arrived in Paris and his mission got off to an unpromising start. Franklin might have received a celebrity's welcome from most of the French, but the ambassadors with whom he was scheduled to meet canceled some of their initial sessions with him, came late to others, and when they did show up seemed inattentive and impatient for the sessions to end. They didn't believe the Americans could win the war, even though it was on their own soil, and despite being foes of the British themselves, the French did not want to invest their money in a cause that seemed so unlikely to offer a worthwhile return.

But as the Americans began to prove themselves on the battlefield, especially with their defeat of the British at Saratoga in September 1777, the French began to warm to Franklin's pleas. By the summer of 1778, he, like the colonial forces, was making undeniable progress; the French, he was certain, were beginning to feel the same confidence that he did in an American victory. Still, the going was slow, and the French remained reluctant to make as serious a commitment as Franklin had been urging.

The attitudes of his fellow negotiators also hampered him, he complained. Franklin believed that Ralph Izard and Arthur Lee resented the fact that, by congressional mandate, they were serving as subordinates to Franklin, not equals. They not only behaved boorishly toward him and did the work he assigned them grudgingly, if at all, but actually went so far, Franklin charged, as to conspire against him to the detriment of America's position in the talks. So adamant was Franklin in this belief that he even resorted to a soupçon of modesty in his accusation: "If ever any Man was most cordially hated and detested by Persons whom he never desired to offend, I am so by two of our Countrymen here, for which I can give no kind of Account, unless it be that I am too much respected, complimented and caress'd by the People in general, and a Deference a little too particular paid me by some in Power, the whole indeed far above my Merit, but which I do not seek and cannot help."

The following year both Lee and Izard were recalled to America. Franklin toasted their departure. But one of their replacements was John Adams, whose jealousy of Franklin made Lee and Izard seem like the most generous spirits of the age.

Before Adams fumed at Franklin for his negotiating style in Paris, he had fussed at him for the way he slept in America. In 1776, with Franklin long since having been a celebrity and Adams still a bit player, the two men were on their way to a summit meeting of sorts with British admiral Lord Richard Howe, who supposedly had a plan to end the war. The Americans doubted the plan would favor them, believing the Crown would make no concessions. But they decided there would be no harm in listening. If nothing else, they could demonstrate their commitment to independence by rejecting Howe's proposal and storming out of the room.

Stopping for the night at an inn in New Brunswick, New Jersey, Franklin and Adams found it so crowded that were told they could be accommodated only if they shared a bed. Reluctantly they agreed. The result, as Franklin biographer Walter Isaacson observes, "was a somewhat farcical night."

As they prepared to retire, Adams shut the window. Franklin told him to open it, lest they suffocate. Adams said he had a cold and did not want to make it worse. Franklin said the night air would make Adams feel better, not worse. Franklin had worked out a theory about colds — how they developed, how they were transmitted — and was happy to share it with his roommate. You can imagine Adams shaking his head and muttering: Franklin has a theory about *everything*!

He explained. Colds "may possibly be spread by contagion," Franklin stated, not low temperatures. He told Adams that he had often felt the sting of bitter winter weather, but had caught colds only "when shut up together in close rooms, etc., and when sitting near and conversing so as to breathe in each other's transpiration." An open window, Franklin said, would clear the air and improve the chances of regaining a salubrious state.

Adams, as he later wrote, listened to Franklin's "harrangue" as long as he could, but not as long as Franklin might have wished, as "I was so much amused," he said, "that I soon fell asleep, and left him and his philosophy together."

Franklin opened the window and it stayed open all night. Adams's cold did not get worse. "The next Morning We proceeded on our Journey," Adams wrote, without further comment.

Adams's feelings toward Franklin, however, did worsen. Two years later in Paris circumstances again forced them to share quarters, but each lived in a separate world when it came to one's view of the other's merits. Some of it could not be helped. Adams was three decades younger than his fellow ambassador. There was no way for them to see eye to eye.

But Adams was in a bad mood before he even laid eyes Franklin. No sooner had he arrived in Paris than the French showered him with ignorance, knowing neither his name nor his contributions to the cause of American independence. They wanted to know whether he was "the famous Adams, *Le fameux Adams?*" That is, Sam Adams, a far rowdier rebel than his cousin, who had thus attracted more notice in the press at home and abroad. Or they meant the author of *Common Sense,* which had so eloquently stated the case for American freedom and which a number of Frenchmen believed had been written by someone named Adams rather than Thomas Paine. John Adams was constantly shaking his head in his first days in Paris: *No, I'm not Sam. No,* I didn't write *Common Sense.* It was a far cry from the reception that Franklin received when he arrived in the French capital, and Adams, all too aware of the difference, seethed.

Working with Franklin only made matters worse. Adams believed that Franklin was indolent in his efforts to enlist French support — late for meetings himself, not two-fisted enough in his approach. Franklin cared too much about soaking up attention, Adams concluded, not enough about the colorless, crucial work of reaching accord on the myriad small matters that negotiations encompassed. It was almost the same charge that Livingston had made against Adams in the Netherlands. "A man must be his own trumpeter," Adams wrote disparagingly of Franklin. "He must write or dictate paragraphs of praise in the newspapers, he must dress, have a retinue and equipage, he must ostentatiously publish in the world his own writings with his name, write even panegyrics on them, he must get his picture drawn, his statue made, and must hire all the artists in his turn, to set about works to spread his name, make the mob stare and gape and perpetuate his fame." Adams thought Franklin had mastered this approach to a fault.

As for Franklin, although he tried to tolerate his younger, hot-headed partner, he did not always succeed. He found Adams lacking in the kinds of social skills that were diplomatic skills as well, the kinds of subtle behavior that would lay the groundwork for harmonious negotiations and make the French more likely to accede to American requests. In addition, he found Adams lacking in simple amiability, whether with the French or his fellow Americans.

Adams could sense Franklin's dissatisfaction with him, and bristled at it in the pages of his diary. In a period of five days in the spring of 1778, he recorded his resentment three times, and covered a lot of ground in the process.

APRIL 16: "Dr. Franklin was reported to speak french very well, but I found upon attending critically to him that he did not speak it, grammatically. . . . His pronunciation too, upon which the French Gentlemen and Ladies complemented him very highly and which he seemed to think pretty well, I soon found was very inaccurate, and some Gentlemen of high rank afterwards candidly told me that it was so confused, that it was scarcely possible to understand him."

APRIL 19: "I neither then nor ever since suspected any unfair practice in Franklin except some secret whispers against Lee and possibly against myself."

APRIL 21: "That [Franklin] was a great Genius, a great Wit, a great Humourist and a great Satyrist, and a great Politician is certain. That he was a great Phylosopher, a great Moralist and a great Statesman is more questionable."

Franklin must have vexed Adams like no one he had ever known before because, like most others acquainted with the older man, Adams could not help but fall under the spell of his charm from time to time, to wonder at his ease in times of crisis and the vast roster of his achievements — the result of which was that Adams's animus toward Franklin occasionally dropped below its normal levels. For instance, a few days before committing the previous statements to his diary, Adams wrote that he and Franklin had spent "the best part of two Years in Congress in great Harmony and Civility, and there had grown up between Us that kind of Friendship which is commonly felt between two members of the same public Assembly."

Perhaps it pained him to say such a thing. Perhaps not. Perhaps the admission served as an anodyne, calming Adams when his jealousies were threatening to roil out of control. Regardless, to read Adams's comments about Franklin over a period of several decades is to conclude that he was far more in character indicting the eldest of the founders than praising him. He accused Franklin of having "a Passion for Reputation and Fame, as strong as you can imagine, and his Time and Thoughts are chiefly employed to obtain it, and to set Tongues and Pens, male and female, to celebrating him." Of course, Adams would not have minded being a bit more *fameux* himself.

Ultimately, he decided that Franklin in France was "a great philosopher, but as a legislator of America he had done very little. It is universally believed in France, England and all Europe that his electric wand has accomplished all this revolution, but nothing is more groundless. He has done very little. It is believed that he made all the American constitutions, and their confederation. But he made neither. He did not even make the constitution of Pennsylvania, bad as it is."

The passage is preposterous, showing Adams at his worst, his pen getting the better of his reason. But his feelings about Franklin were not an aberration. Adams found something to envy in virtually all the founders, most likely something he feared was lacking in himself, some quality or attitude he wanted to possess and did not, or believed he did but could not get others to notice and appreciate. He wanted people to think highly of him. When they did, he suspected them of insincerity.

Adams might have been even more jealous of Washington than he was of Franklin, although not as often, as bitterly, or as personally. Such a mismatched pair they were — Washington with the bearing of a man whose natural perch seemed a pedestal, Adams giving the impression of a clerk whose means were modest and unlikely to improve. One's reputation held so strong that criticism could not affect it, the other's seemed subject to the vicissitudes of daily life. The one who cared less about fame had accumulated enough of it to last forever, while the one who cared more could never be certain of his share and performed all sorts of mental gymnastics, many of which he committed to paper, to rationalize his doubts. As the first president and vice president of the United States, they were the éminence grise of nationhood and his hop-along sidekick. And that, it seems certain, was the root of Adams's disenchantment.

Adams respected Washington, even admired him. Adams had nominated the general to be commander in chief of the Continental Army. When the nomination was confirmed, Adams wrote to his wife proudly, "I can now inform you that the Congress have made Choice of the modest and virtuous, the amiable, generous and brave George Washington, Esqr., to be the General of the American Army, and that he is to repair as soon as possible to the Camp before Boston. This Appointment will have a great Effect, in cementing and securing the Union of these Colonies."

Two years later, when Washington was negotiating an exchange of prisoners and the British general with whom he met began to make unforeseen demands, Adams again offered his support. "Washington is in the Right," he informed Abigail, "and has maintained his Argument with a Delicacy, and a Dignity, which do him much Honour."

But there was distance between them at this point in their careers — Washington on a battlefield somewhere and later at Mount Vernon, Adams in a legislative chamber or at a negotiating table in a foreign country. As a result, Adams had no reason to make direct comparisons between himself and the great man. Different categories of endeavor separated them — one a military man, the other a diplomat, each doing his best for independence.

But then they filled the two highest offices in the land. Proximity entered their relationship, and for Adams it was a slow-acting poison. In 1789, as vice president, he found himself with little to do but watch Washington rule the roost. They attended meetings together, but Washington and his cabinet presided. They discussed policy, but Washington made the final decisions, usually after consulting Hamilton, not Adams. They attended the same social functions, but Washington was the cynosure of attention. They stood side by side, which forced Adams to look up to Washington figuratively and literally. Entombed within the damp walls of the vice presidency, Adams had too much time not only to think about their differences but, worse, to note the ways in which others reacted to those differences. He could not help but be envious.

Adams didn't reveal his feelings for many years, not until Washington had died and Adams himself had surrendered the presidency to Jefferson and those who followed him — but it was when Washington and Adams bridged the gap between them by heading the new national government that a gulf of a different kind began to form. When it was finally made public, it dealt a blow to Adams's reputation that history would have a hard time forgiving.

In those days political parties, as we understand the term, didn't exist. There were no tickets on election day, with one man running for president and a partner applying for the second spot, the two of them a team of united purpose. Instead, several men sought the highest office, with the electors' favorite winning the office and the runner-up getting the consolation prize. It seemed fair, democratic, a means of ensuring that the two most competent or at least popular of the candidates would fill the top two positions in the nation's government.

The flaw in the thinking did not become apparent until the third presidential election. In the first two, with Washington leading the polls and Adams trailing, the offices went to men of similar political persuasion. Both were Federalists, not only believing in a strong central government but, in foreign affairs, insisting that the United

States was a more natural ally of England than of France. They agreed on most matters of governance and economics, and when they didn't, the differences between them were in virtually all cases minor. There were no intrigues. There was no backstabbing.

But in the third election, Adams garnered the most votes and Jefferson finished second, resulting in a mixed marriage of the worst kind, a relationship doomed from the start.

The most controversial issue of the Adams presidency was the French Revolution. Adams tried to continue Washington's policy of neutrality while privately decrying the bloody excesses of the Jacobins, France's antimonarchists. Jefferson, on the other hand, saw the Jacobins as the same kind of patriots that the American colonists had been, and thought his countrymen should support them, rooting for the overthrow of the monarchy no matter how many times the blade of the guillotine dropped and how much blood was spilled.

Almost as controversial were the Alien and Sedition Acts, which in the first case allowed the president to imprison or deport foreigners if he thought them a threat to American security, and in the second allowed the government to censor the press. Adams supported the acts hesitantly, aware of their dictatorial nature but pleased to have such weapons at hand — especially the Sedition Act, which allowed him to avenge himself against opposition newspapers that excoriated him. Jefferson couldn't have disagreed more. He thought that both acts were an affront to all that America stood for and encouraged popular and judicial resistance against them.

In the next election, Jefferson defeated Adams for the presidency, limiting him to a single term and causing his disagreements with Jefferson to flare into jealousy.

Adams and Jefferson had been friends in the years leading up to the Revolutionary War, each respecting the other and working together without argument — but even then the occasional sign of discord appeared. "Mr. Jefferson had been now about a Year a member of Congress," Adams wrote later, "but had attended his Duty in the House but a very small part of the time and when there had never spoken in public; and during the whole time I sat with him in Congress, I never heard him utter three Sentences together. The most of a Speech he ever made in my hearing was a gross insult on Religion, in one or two Sentences, for which I gave him immediately the Reprehension, which he richly merited."

For the most part, Adams regarded Jefferson highly, certainly during the war, when each believed the other was doing his best to advance colonial goals. A few years later, though, Adams grew wary of Jefferson again, thinking him something of a spy in Washington's camp. He was right. Serving as Washington's secretary of state, Jefferson not only found many of the president's policies misguided but helped to create a newspaper, the *National Gazette*, that publicized the Republican opposition to those policies. Jefferson provided money for the *Gazette*, and leaked information to the editor so he could denounce the very administration in which he was a leading figure. Some of that money came from the State Department's own budget!

Adams didn't know all the details, but he knew that the secretary was working against the president's interests, and so was relieved when Jefferson decided he had had enough of the State Department and would return to private life. "I have so long been in the habit of thinking well of his Abilities and general good dispositions," Adams wrote to Abigail at the time, "that I cannot but feel some regret at this Event: but his want of Candour, his obstinate Prejudices both of Aversion and Attachment, his real Partiality in Spite of all his Pretensions, and his low notions about many things have so nearly reconciled me to it, that I will not weep."

A few days later, when Jefferson had actually packed his belongings and removed himself from Philadelphia, heading back to Monticello for yet another short-lived retirement, Adams pronounced "a good riddance of bad ware. I hope his Temper will be more cool and his Principles more reasonable in Retirement than they have been in office. I am almost tempted to wish he may be chosen Vice President at the next Election for there if he could do no good, he could do no harm."

Jefferson would not be chosen vice president until the election after that, however, and Adams, as his superior, would rue the electors' decision from the moment they made it.

But Jefferson proved not to be the real bane of the Adams administration. As vice president, he could skulk in a corner with other Republicans and hiss at Adams's initiatives, but his rank limited his power, and his newspaper had gone out of business a few years earlier. There were other Republican journals, but Jefferson did not control them. He could do no real harm.

Alexander Hamilton, however, could — even though he had left the government, stepping down as secretary of the treasury early in 1795 and becoming a lawyer in private practice, probably more prosperous than Adams had ever been. Never comfortable with Hamilton's aggressive nature, Adams was even more pleased at his departure than at Jefferson's.

But was Hamilton really gone?

Even before taking over the presidency, Adams had an important decision to make: should he hold onto Washington's cabinet or dismiss its members and bring in men of his own choosing? He could see advantages and disadvantages to both alternatives, but finally determined to keep the incumbents. It made for a smoother, more efficient transition, he concluded, and thus would be the better option for a country still in its infancy, one that needed to be rocked gently in its cradle.

Adams realized his mistake almost immediately. The men in the leftover cabinet were more loyal to Hamilton, as Washington's proxy, than they were to Washington's successor, an electorally mandated successor. Hamilton had been a much more trusted ally of the first president than Adams. It was he, after all, who had conferred with Washington on his most important decisions and had continued to draft his speeches as chief executive just as he had done during the war, knowing so well his leader's voice, sentiments, and convictions.

Some of Adams's cabinet officials corresponded with Hamilton. Some began to meet with him in secret, seeking advice about issues under consideration and then trying to promote Hamiltonian notions in Congress. Some didn't cast their votes until they had received Hamilton's approval. Some couldn't forgive Adams for not being Washington.

Hamilton had figured out a way to make his presence felt, and Adams both despised and envied him for commanding loyalty among the cabinet he couldn't command himself. Abigail Adams had been right. Hamilton wanted to be president. To a degree that appalled the Adamses, he had succeeded.

As was the case with Jefferson, Adams had seen the problems coming. In 1795, watching Hamilton at the Treasury Department, the vice president bridled not only at his vanity but, after one especially contentious meeting with Washington's top advisers, at the path down which he seemed to be leading his fellow Americans. "Hamilton has made of a whole Nation a Stockjobbing, Speculating, selfish People," Adams wrote to his wife. "Riches alone here see consideration; and as no one likes to be despised they are universally sought after. Nevertheless this depravity has not yet embraced the Mob of the People, &c." And shortly before he became president, Adams declared: "Hamilton I know to be a proud Spirited, conceited, aspiring Mortal always pretending to Morality, with as debauched Morals as old Franklin who is more his Model than any one I know. As great an Hypocrite as any in the U.S."

There was a time during the Adams administration when it seemed that the United States might be going to war with England again, since both parties were ignoring the terms of the Treaty of Paris. It didn't happen, but Adams began to prepare for the possibility — discussing military strategy with former officers of Washington's army, soliciting advice on raising and funding a new fighting force, and preparing a case for Congress.

And hearing pleas from Hamilton. Eager as ever for military action, Hamilton told Adams he would consider it an honor to serve his country again, would happily assume any command the president granted him, and would meet his responsibilities with utmost conscientiousness.

What Adams said to Hamilton, if anything, we don't know. What he said to himself is obvious. Adams would never consider granting so despised a foe the chance for glory. Hamilton was "the most restless, impatient, artful, indefatigable and unprincipled intriguer in the United States, if not in the world," Adams believed, and he would see to it that the man remained a civilian no matter how great the nation's need for military leadership.

Three decades earlier — before Adams had been thrown into collaboration and conflict with Franklin, Washington, Jefferson, and Hamilton — a ship called the *Liberty* had sailed into Boston Harbor, its hold full of Madeira wine. Among those watching it dock were a British customs officer, waiting to collect taxes on the cargo, and the ship's owner, John Hancock, who had no intention of paying those taxes. When the customs officer approached Hancock and demanded that he hand over the money, Hancock ordered his crewmen to grab the officer, lock him up in the ship's cabin, and keep him there until the vessel was unloaded and the men had managed a safe departure. We don't know how long the customs officer remained confined, only that he swore revenge on his captor as soon as he was free again.

From that point on, John Hancock became a leading figure in the American struggle for independence.

The following year, he was elected to the Massachusetts legislature. In 1770, he became head of the Boston Town Committee and after that the president of the Massachusetts Provincial Congress. In all of these positions he criticized British policies and encouraged his fellow colonists to think, and eventually govern, for themselves. So upset were the British about Hancock's statements, many of which were reprinted in newspapers and pamphlets, that in 1775, about the time the Revolutionary War began, they tried to arrest him and his fellow rebel, Sam Adams. Paul Revere, who would issue a more famous warning later that year, now warned Hancock and Adams that the British were coming for them, and the two men were able to escape.

Hancock served as president of the Second Continental Congress, and was the first of fifty-six Americans to sign the Declaration of Independence, writing his name bigger and more boldly than the others. When asked why, he is supposed to have said that he wanted George III to see it all the way across the Atlantic, even without his glasses, and therefore to know that the colonists stood large and united in their opposition to him.

All of which were reasons for John Adams to have been favorably disposed to Hancock. And there were more. Hancock's father, a noted clergyman, had baptized Adams in 1735. As children, Adams and Hancock were playmates in Braintree, running heedlessly through the village on summer days, inventing games that annoyed their elders, and perhaps taking a break once in a while to lie under a tree and wonder what the future would bring for them.

Later, Hancock hired Adams as his lawyer, and Adams served him well in a number of cases, most of them minor business matters. Adams's "account with John Hancock, for instance," writes Adams biographer James Grant, "covering the period March 1769 to December 1771, shows 25 different items in 19 separate actions, footing up to a grand billable total of £55." When their business relationship ended, Adams was disappointed but not surprised. He assumed his client's legal affairs were now so well organized that he had no further need for counsel.

Yet Adams eventually turned on Hancock, too. It was as if he were warming up for his later resentments against the other founders. Adams claimed that he "saw in Mr. Hancock and Mr. Samuel Adams very visible marks of jealousy and Envy too," and that the reason — or one of them, at least — was the relationship Adams had developed with a Major Joseph Hawley. At the time, Hancock, Hawley, and both Adamses were serving on a committee to draft a reply to the British after Parliament claimed that it, and not the citizens of Massachusetts, had the right to name judges for the colony. Nonsense, thought the citizens, and the committee formed to express their indignation.

As it labored over a response, Hawley developed a higher opinion of John Adams than he did of Sam or Hancock. The latter two knew it and, John believed, did not take it well. Still, he said, "I regarded it very little, and it made no Alteration in my respectful and friendly behaviour toward them."

But it did make an alteration that Adams expressed on more than one occasion. Many years later, after both his cousin and Hancock had died, Adams still remembered their supposed alliance against him and wrote about it in his autobiography. The two men, he claimed, "indulged their jealousies so far as to cooperate in dissiminating Prejudices against me, as a Monarchy Man and a Friend to England, for which I hope they have been forgiven, in Heaven as I have constantly forgiven them on Earth, though they both knew the insinuations were groundless." It was a long time to carry so inconsequential, and perhaps even ill-founded, a grudge.

Initially supporting Hancock as president of the Second Continental Congress, Adams soon found fault with him. Like Hamilton, Adams concluded, Hancock was promoting his own interests at the expense of the colonies as a whole, unwilling to acknowledge the contributions of others. And, Adams decided, he was too sensitive. Hancock had hoped that he himself, not Washington, would lead the American military effort against the British, and could not forgive Adams for nominating the Congress's ultimate choice. Adams had done it, Hancock seems to have believed, out of a spite that had no basis in fact. Despite a certain regard for Hancock, Adams thought Washington the better man for the job.

Differing views of military actions to be taken during the Revolutionary War led to further rifts between Adams and Hancock. The latter found fault with Washington's every move, while Adams offered almost unqualified support. The two of them disagreed, for instance, on how the colonial troops should have comported themselves at the battle of Bunker Hill. We don't know the specifics of the quarrel, only that Adams thought it had a significant impact on Hancock's feelings toward him. "Mr. Hancock . . . never loved me so well after this Event as he had done before," Adams claimed, "and he made me feel at times the Effects of his resentment and of his jealousy in many Ways and at diverse times, as long as he lived, though at other times according to his variable feelings, he even overacted his part in professing his regard and respect to me."

Later, and more broadly, Adams had written to his wife, "Jealousy is as cruel as the Grave, and Envy as spightfull as Hell — and neither have any regard to Veracity or Honour." It takes a man who is well acquainted with jealousy himself to find so much of it directed at him by others.

In time, Adams mellowed. But before that, he fulminated even more, and the man to whom he would most often reveal his ongoing rancor was, ironically, one of the most gracious of the founders, one of the few who called the majority of the others his friends.

Second only to Franklin among men of his generation, Benjamin Rush was a man of versatile accomplishment and indiscriminate inquisitiveness. He was not only the leading physician of the colonial era, serving the Continental Army as surgeon general, but also came to be known as the father of American psychiatry. He was a congressman, a delegate to the First Continental Congress, and a signer of the Declaration of Independence. He cofounded both the Philadelphia Bible Society and Dickinson College. He was the first American seriously to oppose alcohol and tobacco. His early writings led to reform movements for both substances, not to mention derision on the part of their more fervent users. Rush financed a school for children of African descent and helped establish the first formal group of abolitionists in the United States — all this in addition to studying a broad variety of topics, from agriculture and astronomy to human and animal migration patterns.

And from 1805 to 1813, Rush corresponded faithfully with John Adams, the two of them exchanging letters in which Adams was often exorcising demons more than relaying information. Some of the letters show Adams at his most self-pityingly splenetic, dismissing one former colleague after another as he marched through the years, raining down vituperation like an angry god.

AUGUST 23, 1805, looking back on two of the founders after they had died, Adams wrote: "You say that Washington and Hamilton are idolized by the tories. Hamilton is; Washington is not. To speak the truth, they puffed Washington like an air balloon to raise Hamilton into the air. . . . Hamilton's talents have been greatly exaggerated. His knowledge of the great subjects of coin and commerce and their intimate connections with all departments of every government, especially such as are so elective as ours, was very superficial and imperfect. . . . I see no extraordinary reason for so much exclusive glory to Hamilton."

SEPTEMBER 30, 1805, upset that Hamilton and Jefferson had not given him enough credit for suggesting to the Second Continental Congress that the colonies send ambassadors to France, and afraid that Rush would criticize him for being so sensitive about it, Adams said: "All of this you will call vanity and egotism. Such indeed it is. But Jefferson and Hamilton ought not to steal from me my good name and rob me of the reputation of a system which I was born to introduce, 'refin'd it first and show'd its use,' as really as Dean Swift did irony."

JULY 23, 1806, bemoaning the quality of political discourse at the time, implying that modern practitioners were not as eloquent as they had been in the days leading up to war, Adams sneered: "Oratory in this age? Secrecy! Cunning! Silence! *Voilà les grands sciences des* *temps modernes*[*] Washington! Franklin! Jefferson! Eternal silence! impenetrable secrecy! deep cunning! These are the talents and virtues which are triumphant in these days."

FEBRUARY 25, 1808, annoyed at the continuing adulation for George Washington even though his death was almost a decade past, Adams complained: "When my parson says, 'Let us sing to the praise and glory of G.W.,' your church will adopt a new collect in its liturgy and say 'Sancte Washington, ora pro nobis.' "[†]

JUNE 21, 1811, after beginning his letter in a chatty, convivial manner, then warning Rush that "I shall turn my thoughts from this good-humored small talk to the angry, turbulent, stormy science of politics," Adams did indeed turn turbulent: "The Declaration of Independence I always considered as a theatrical show. Jefferson ran away with all the stage effect of that . . . and all the glory of it." And why? Adams, after all, had come up with the idea for such a document long before. "I think I may boast of my [own] declaration of independence in 1755," he moaned, "twenty-one years older than this."

JULY 8, 1812, it was back to Washington, as Adams informed Rush: "I ought to have mentioned in my last letter the idolatrous worship paid to the name of General Washington by all classes and *nearly* all parties of our citizens, manifested in the impious application of names and epithets to him which are ascribed in Scripture only to God and to Jesus Christ. The following is a part of them: 'our Saviour,' 'our Redeemer,' 'our cloud by day and our pillar of fire by night,' 'our star in the east,' 'to us a Son is born,' and 'our guide on earth, our advocate in Heaven.' "

---

[*]"These are the great sciences of modern times."
[†]"Saint Washington, pray for us."

There were times between 1805 and 1813 when Adams's jealousies seemed more than he could bear, when he felt so sorry for himself that he lapsed into fantasy to justify his irrationalities, to lament the course of his life, which needed far less lamenting than most. Perhaps the saddest of all the passages in the Rush–Adams letters, and the most taxing on the recipient's patience, is the following, which Adams wrote in 1809:

> I am weary, my friend, of that unceasing insolence of which I have been the object for twenty years. I have opposed nothing to it but stoical patience, unlimited submission, passive obedience, and non-resistance. Mausoleums, statues, monuments will never be erected to me. I wish them not. Panegyrical romances will never be written, nor flattering orations spoken, to transmit me to posterity in brilliant colors. No, nor in true colors. All but the last I loathe. Yet I will not die wholly unlamented. Cicero was libeled, slandered, insulted by all parties. . . . He was persecuted and tormented by turns by all parties and all factions and that for his most virtuous and glorious actions. In his anguish at times . . . he was driven to those assertions of his own actions which have been denominated vanity. Instead of reproaching them with vanity, I think them the most infallible demonstration of his innocence and purity. He declares that all honors are indifferent to him because he knows that it is not in the power of his country to reward him in any proportion to his Services.

It might have been true of Cicero, but Adams is of course writing about himself here as much as he is the legendary Roman. This man who had started out his career so many years earlier fearing he would never achieve the fame he deserved ended up achieving it all, yet never conquering the fear.

During these years, ironically, Adams began to mellow, as if his increased vitriol in some of the letters to Rush acted as a safety valve, releasing enough pressure so that he could be more charitable, indulging his better nature, in other messages.

By 1809 many of the Founding Fathers had died, not just Washington and Hamilton but Franklin, Hancock, Henry, Sam Adams, and a number of others. The two most famous survivors were Adams himself and Jefferson. Rush, who thought highly of both, believed that deep inside the two of them wanted to regain the friendship of their early days but, paralyzed by pride, could not bring themselves to take the necessary steps. Jefferson would not write to Adams, doubtful that Adams would write back, and Adams feared being ignored or, worse, insulted by Jefferson. The impasse seemed insurmountable, but Rush set out to break it.

On October 17, he suggested that Adams send a short note to Jefferson, just a few lines, the written equivalent of a hello in passing at a social event. Adams hesitated. Rush then confided to him that he had had a dream the previous night, and that dreams were not to be dismissed by wakeful minds. Rush's medical training had taught him that they were, rather, important clues to the truest nature of a man, capable of providing "useful inferences."

Adams told him to go on.

In his dream, Rush said, Adams had written a letter to Jefferson, congratulating him on his retirement from the presidency. Jefferson had written back, delighted to have heard from his old mate. From that point, the correspondence between the two men continued for many years, tentatively at first, then with increasing frequency and at ever greater length. Adams listened attentively to Rush's tale, perhaps even enjoying it. But he remained unwilling to pick up his pen.

Rush does not seem to have told Jefferson of his dream, but he did encourage him to send a letter, however brief, to Adams. He assured Jefferson that Adams would look kindly on it. But Jefferson would not make the first move, either. Rush's dream, for the time being at least, remained just that.

Not until more than two years had passed, on January 1, 1812, did the lines of communication finally open, with Adams writing to

Jefferson, wishing him a happy new year and many more. He brought up nothing of greater substance. It was the equivalent of that hello in passing. But Jefferson was delighted with the overture and responded warmly and promptly. "A letter from you calls up recollections very dear to my mind," he wrote. "It carried me back to the times when, beset with difficulties and dangers, we were fellow laborers in the same cause, struggling for what is most valuable to man, his right of self-government."

With that, the friendship renewed, Rush's dream at last becoming a reality, and the correspondence became so warm that Adams closed one of his letters: "You may expect, many more expostulations from one who has loved and esteemed you for Eight and thirty years."

Adams and Jefferson never saw each other again, but they continued to exchange letters for the rest of their lives, and both men treasured the dispatches of their last years. They were apart but together again, companions of the sort they had been so long ago, and even when they did broach contentious matters on which they had previously disagreed, they did so civilly, each respecting the other's point of view, each revealing an understanding he had not revealed, or felt, in the past, each apologizing for having offended in those bygone times. Jefferson to Adams on one such topic: "I have thus stated my opinion on a point on which we differ, not with a view to controversy, for we are both too old to change opinions, which are the result of a long line of inquiry and reflection; but on the suggestion of a former letter of yours, that we ought not to die before we have explained ourselves to each other."

The year before Adams and Jefferson began writing to each other, Adams displayed what might have been an even more remarkable change of heart in an essay for a Boston newspaper called the *Patriot*. He did not forgive his subject for what he still believed to be the shortcomings of his lifetime, nor did he apologize for the previous statements he had made against him. But he obviously believed that he had something to argue for, and he set about it with as much sincerity as he had previously mustered to denigrate the man.

> Franklin had a great genius, original, sagacious and inventive, capable of discoveries in science no less than of improvement in the fine arts and the mechanical arts. He had a vast imagination. . . . He had wit at will. He had a humor that, when he pleased, was delicate and delightful. He had a satire that was good-natured or caustic, Horace or Juvenal, Swift or Rabelais, at his pleasure. He had talents for irony, allegory and fable that he could adapt with great skill to the promotion of moral and political truth. He was master of that infantile simplicity which the French call naivete, which never fails to charm.

Perhaps, it would be lovely to believe, Adams had finally reached a stage in his life, with a decade and a half left of it, at which his pride in his own achievements was substantial enough to admit to a pride in others.

Chapter 8
Image

ADAMS DID NOT LIKE POSING FOR PORTRAITS any more than he liked sleeping with the windows open. He knew that lasting fame required lasting images and that marble busts of Cicero had survived more than a millennium — but that didn't make the process any easier. It tired Adams both physically and emotionally, sitting for all those hours, maintaining a posture as unflattering as it was uncomfortable, as well as maintaining a facade of interest in the incessant chattering of the artist. Sometimes, Adams thought, painters treated him more like a captive audience for their blather than as a subject for their vocation. "Speaking generally," he said near the end of his life, "no penance is like having one's picture done."

Unless, that is, the picture was being done by Charles Willson Peale, whom Adams believed was "ingenious." Further, he "has Vanity — loves Finery — Wears a sword — gold Lace — speaks French." In other words, Peale appealed to the elitist in Adams.

Or unless the painter was Gilbert Stuart, another favorite of Adams and one of the most esteemed artists of the era. Born in

Rhode Island, Stuart had been the toast of London for more than a decade, then returned to America for further acclaim, in no small part because of a portrait of George Washington that he never finished. Stuart impressed Adams with his tongue as well as his brush. He "lets me do just what I please," Adams said, "and keeps me constantly amused by his conversation."

Of many other artists Adams did not think as highly. Nor did he think, despite his desire to leave behind a visual record of himself, that the time was right for him to be memorialized either on canvas or in stone. "The age of sculpture and painting has not yet arrived in this country," he declared, "and I hope it will not arrive very soon. Artists have done what they pleased with my face and eyes, head and shoulders, stature and figure and they have made of them monsters as fit for exhibition as Harlequin or Punch."

It was not the only time Adams complained about his treatment at the hands of those whose charge was to reproduce him faithfully. "Sir," he wrote to his friend, the Philadelphia publisher Joseph Delaplaine, "There are several things abroad which are reported to have been intended as pictures of me; some of them drawn by persons who never saw me, others by persons to whom I never sat and others by painters who [never] requested me to sit. I pretend not to be a judge of the merit of any of them. But there is not an approved likeness among them. . . . My head has been so long the sport of painters, as my heart has been of libellers, that I shall make no objection to any use that may be made of either." His best qualities, Adams believed, were his "candor, probity, and decision." Seldom did he see any of these conveyed on canvas.

Motivated by "no small amount of vanity" — the phrase comes from art historian David Meschutt — Adams sat for more than two dozen portraits in his life. The whole Adams family, especially John Quincy, the sixth American president, obsessed over their likenesses: how they were drawn, where they were shown, who would see them, what those people would think.

The leading artists of the day painted Adams, not just Stuart and

Peale but John Singleton Copley and John Trumbull. And such a vet eran model did Adams become that he dared to tell Trumbull how to do his job. Shortly before the two were to collaborate, Adams wrote to him, admitting that "I have taken the liberty of friendship to preach to you." At least the sermon was brief. "Truth, nature, fact, should be your sole guide," Adams said to Trumbull, who had not asked for advice and was surely not pleased to receive it from someone who had never held a palette or mixed a color in his life. "Let not our posterity be deluded with fictions under the pretense of poetical or graphical license." Trumbull had proposed a large painting. Adams thought a smaller one would be better. "The dimensions, eighteen by twelve, appear vast. . . . I have been informed that one of the greatest talents of a painter is a capacity to comprehend a large space, and to proportion all his figures in it."

About the making of life masks, however, Adams offered no guidance. The procedure was not as lengthy as sitting for a portrait, but was in its own way more painful and sometimes even frightening, especially for those who put themselves in the hands of sculptor John Henry Browere. "Instead of lying flat on the back," writes art historian Everett L. Millar, "Browere's subjects posed in a semi-reclining position. The artist oiled the skin, greased the eyebrows and hair, and stuck straws in the nostrils." Then the victim's face was covered with several layers of a thin grout, the ingredients of which Browere, proud of his secret formula, revealed to no one. The substance remained in place until dry, which usually took about twenty minutes, during which time the subject breathed through the straws and tried to persuade himself that he wasn't being buried alive.

After the allotted time, Browere carefully removed the plaster, tapping it lightly a few times with a hammer so it would come off in a few large pieces. Then he glued the pieces together to make a mold into which he poured either plaster or bronze to form the mask, which was supposed to be an accurate representation of the person from the shoulders up.

Often, however, it was not. Often the mask showed its subject grimacing or scowling — not because the artist had captured the subject's true nature, but because the sitter had been suffering the unpleasantness of wearing a mask of wet grout as it hardened.

Adams didn't want to submit to a life mask. He especially didn't want to submit to Browere, who seemed not altogether trustworthy to him. But John Quincy had had a life mask done by Browere a few years earlier and assured his father that the finished product was worth the inconvenience. Furthermore, he said, Browere was hoping to build a gallery that would house the life masks of early America's most prominent figures, and it would hardly be complete without John Adams. Adams agreed.

The year before he died, he told Browere he was ready. The sculptor came and worked his craft on Adams, who seems to have found the mask a reasonable likeness. If only there had been some other way to make it. "He did not tear my face to pieces," Adams wrote of the sculptor shortly after the session, "though I sometimes thought he would beat my brains out with his hammer."

Adams continued to doubt that generations to come would remember him, or if they did, that they would remember him fondly. But he also continued to hope. He had long since left behind a list of achievements that he believed to be significant, reinforced by all manner of likenesses. If posterity wanted to reflect on John Adams, if it wanted to know who he was, what he had done, and how his actions had influenced the times in which he had lived, not to mention how he carried himself, it would have every opportunity.

More than a quarter of a century after Adams's death, Thomas Carlyle explained what motivated not only the second president but all the founders who bequeathed to the future their images as well as their deeds:

> Every student and reader of History who strives earnestly to conceive for himself what manner of Fact and *Man* this or the other vague Historical *Name* can have been, will, as the first and directest indication of all, search eagerly for a Portrait, for all the

reasonable Portraits there are; and never rest till he have made out, if possible, what the man's natural face was like. Often I have found a Portrait superior in real instruction to half-a-dozen written 'Biographies,' as Biographies are written; — or rather, let me say, I have found that the Portrait was a small lighted *candle* by which the Biographies could for the first times be *read*, and some human interpretation be made of them.

Jefferson had a worse time with Browere than Adams did, yielding to his entreaties, as with Adams, near the end of his life, and perhaps even believing that Browere had been appointed by the fates specifically to bring his life to a close.

In the process of making a life mask of that amiable but elderly gentleman, Browere, after covering his head and neck with plaster, left it there for an hour instead of the twenty minutes that had been expected. The plaster became so hard that a chisel and mallet were required for its removal. Though the victim afterwards made light of the danger and suffering, he emitted groans in the course of this operation, and his daughter and granddaughters feared that he would suffocate. Since the girls expressed themselves indignantly to others as well as to the sculptor, the story got out, to the injury of his reputation. To offset this Jefferson afterwards gave him a testimonial.

Friends gave him testimonials, too. The mask was said by one of them to have been a "perfect facsimile," and by another to have been "a faithful and living Likeness." Jefferson's granddaughter Virginia, however, did not care how the mask looked; to her, Browere was, and would remain, a "vile plasterer."

Jefferson had better luck with painters, and again like Adams, is said to have posed for them more than two dozen times between the ages of forty-three and eighty-three, and to have been captured in virtually all existing media — "wax, plaster, and marble, and executed in oil, gouache, crayon, and gold leaf on canvas, wood, paper, and glass." When it was proposed that Thomas Sully paint him for the new United States Military Academy, Jefferson eagerly agreed. "I am duly sensible of the honor proposed in giving my portrait a place among the benefactors of our nation," he wrote, "and of the establishment of West Point in particular."

Jefferson also sat for John Trumbull, although he did not presume to give him instruction. Jefferson boasted that the two of them "had been on terms of confidence" for some time, which was precisely the kind of relationship he tried to cultivate with an artist. Often, before he sat for a portrait, Jefferson would invite the man to dinner; by serving as host to an artist, he meant to ensure a certain degree of comfort when artist and subject got to work in the next few days. He wanted to feel that the man reproducing him on canvas was, if not a friend, at least an acquaintance, someone in whose company he could be himself, and someone who, in turn, felt warmly disposed toward him. He believed that the sitting would be less troublesome and the image truer, and perhaps more flattering, as a result.

Jefferson seems to have been especially friendly with Gilbert Stuart, for whom he sat a variety of times and whose depiction of Jefferson appears today on postage stamps. Of portraits that Stuart did of him in 1800 and 1805, Stuart preferred the former. Jefferson disagreed, finding the latter more suitable, telling Stuart that it was "a very fine thing," which he "deemed the best which has been taken of me."

But Jefferson did not always have opinions about the paintings for which he sat, and even when he did, they were subject to change. Later, for example, comparing the two paintings by Stuart with a third that Stuart had done, a profile in watercolors to be used to cast medallions, Jefferson admitted how hard it was to be objective: "Of the merit of these I am not a judge," he confessed, "there being nothing to which a man is so incompetent as to judge of his own likeness, he can see himself only by reflection, and that of necessity full-faced or nearly so." And later still, asked by a friend which he thought was the best image of him ever produced, Jefferson could not reply. "I am not qualified to say anything," he had to admit, "for this is a case where the precept of 'know thyself' does not apply." It was not easy, this business of being an art critic, especially when critic and model were the same person.

As a subject, Jefferson was far from ideal. The historian Henry Adams, John's grandson, explains that Jefferson could not be portrayed with "a few broad strokes of the brush . . . only touch by touch with a fine pencil, and the perfection of the likeness depended upon the shifting and uncertain flicker of its semi-transparent shadows." What Adams meant was that, with Jefferson's shifting moods and sometimes contradictory viewpoints, the face in his portraits varied from one artist to the other, from one sitting to the other, almost as if different persons were being painted. The truth of the man was as hard to place on canvas as it was to situate in the mind. "There was no 'standard likeness,' " writes twentieth-century Jefferson scholar Merrill Peterson. "The portraits ranged from Trumbull's towering red-head of 1776 to Bass Otis's gray-haired old man. Moreover, there was a world of difference between the Trumbull and the dignified Mather Brown, though both were painted at the same time, as there was too between the Otis and its near contemporary by Thomas Sully."

Go online and look at the Trumbull, Otis, Brown, Sully, and various other pictures of Jefferson quickly, one right after another. You will see Jefferson transforming himself, changing his mind, even readjusting his persona, right before your eyes.

Mather Brown painted Jefferson in London in 1786 at the request of John and Abigail Adams. William Short, who had been Jefferson's secretary and would become a successful financier, thought the painting awful, that it contained "no feature" that was recognizably Jeffersonian. The original was lost shortly after it was completed, but Brown had made several copies, and one of them found its way into the Adams household, where it hung for almost a century as one of the proudest possessions not only of John and Abigail but of the generations that followed, up to historian Henry Adams and possibly beyond. Whether it remained hanging face out during the long days of the Adams–Jefferson hostilities, we don't know.

Jefferson, who had already commissioned a painting of Washington for himself and purchased busts of Franklin and naval hero John Paul Jones, returned the favor shortly afterward by asking for a portrait of Adams. Adams said he would be pleased to provide one, but only if the results were satisfactory. He would not let Jefferson see him if he turned out yet again to be one of those "monsters as fit for exhibition as Harlequin or Punch." As Abigail explained to Jefferson in a letter, her husband would do his best to avoid such an impression: "Mr. Adams will write you," she told him. "He has not a portrait that he likes to send you. Mr. Trumble [John Trumbull] talks of taking one. If he succeeds better than his Brethren, Mr. Adams will ask your acceptance of it."

Patrick Henry showed little interest in preserving his countenance for the future. He posed in 1788 for a bust by an Italian sculptor traveling through Virginia at the time, but it does not seem to have been Henry's idea. He sat, however reluctantly, at the request of friends who wanted it for public display. Many years later, one of his grandchildren expressed his satisfaction at the work, declaring that it showed the essence of the man, his character, and his perseverance. He was pleased to have it in his possession. Henry's comment on the work, if he made one, is not recorded.

It seems that only three portraits were done of Henry in his lifetime, all in oil, but no one knows whether he actually posed for them. They might have been done by the artists from memory, or perhaps from studying the previously fashioned bust. Neither in his writings nor his speeches does Henry refer to the paintings, or works of art of any sort, contemporary or otherwise. Henry might have become a different kind of man after joining the ranks of the famous, but that's not the same thing as longing for anonymity.

Perhaps he was too busy to sit for artists. Perhaps he had too many things to do that he thought were more important. Or perhaps Henry believed his speeches would keep him alive through generations to come without the need of visual aids, sharing Adams's belief that the arts of painting and sculpture were not yet sufficiently advanced in America.

If any of these is true, it was a risky assumption. It is also precisely what has happened. Henry's words painted a portrait of him that has lasted the ages.

No less mysterious is the case of Alexander Hamilton, who sat for a number of artists in his lifetime, yet was as silent about both the process and the finished products as Henry had been. There are enough renderings of him, however, that posterity can trace his growth and maturation and decline as we today can trace the arc of a man's life through photographs or videos. Hamilton might not have had much to say about his images, but the profusion of them serves as comment enough.

James Sharples painted his family's favorite portrait of Hamilton, capturing him in profile and accentuating the subject's prominent nose and chin in a manner that made him look impervious to mortal threat.

But it was Trumbull who turned out the most famous portrait of Hamilton, a life-size version done in 1791 at the behest of a group of New York merchants who were "desirous of expressing the sense they entertain of the important Services you have rendered your Country." They planned to hang the work in New York's City Hall, and wanted it "to exhib[it] such part of your Political Life as may be most agreeable to yourself."

Hamilton agreed to the painting, but not to the condition. He would pose for Trumbull, he told the merchants, but he wished the portrait to "appear unconnected with any incident of my political life." And so it did. Hamilton looks regal in Trumbull's version, but the setting is generic, a drape hanging partway over an unidentifiable landscape. So many of the incidents in Hamilton's public life were contentious; he no doubt wanted the portrait to be, as its patrons intended, a tribute more than another source of controversy.

Hamilton also sat for a bust by the Italian sculptor Giuseppe Ceracchi, possibly the same man who sculpted Henry in 1788 while journeying through Virginia. In the Roman style, Ceracchi has draped a toga over Hamilton's shoulder and conveyed "a brisk energy and a massive intelligence in his wide brow." Later, Trumbull, who had long waited to paint Hamilton a second time but was unable to schedule a sitting, finally made the portrait — but with the bust, not Hamilton himself, as the model. As it turned out, the two pictures were "a financial godsend" to him.

In 1804 Hamilton agreed to settle his long-standing rivalry with Aaron Burr by meeting him for a duel. The two men faced each other on a July morning atop a cliff overlooking the Hudson River in Weehawken, New Jersey. They did not stand back to back, then step off ten paces. Instead, as the morning sun reflected brightly off the water, they took up positions at an unknown distance from each other. Hamilton donned a pair of spectacles that he might better see his adversary. Burr glared at him and awaited the signal.

When it came, the two men fired, although there are conflicting accounts of who fired first. Hamilton's shot missed Burr, perhaps deliberately. Burr's hit Hamilton in the abdomen above the right hip, and he died the following day. Newspapers surrounded their stories of the event in thick black borders. "The feelings of the whole community are agonized beyond description," cried one friend to his wife. Another believed that "there was as much or more lamentation as when General Washington died."

There was also a sudden and unprecedented demand for Hamilton's likeness. His friends wanted to remember him. Strangers of similar political persuasion wanted to honor him. Perhaps there was even an enemy or two who was now willing to reconsider him or pay tribute to the man's dedication. Trumbull, as he himself put it, "was kept in comfortable employment for some years in turning out replicas of his 2 portraits."

Benjamin Franklin started presenting himself to artists as a relatively young man, recently retired from the printing trade, just beginning to make his name as an inventor and innovator, and not yet a diplomat. As a result, the early portraits reveal a very different figure from the one we know today. As biographer Carl Van Doren writes, Franklin "was not in appearance unmistakably a philosopher. His eyes were open, full, and bold, the line of his mouth straight and even a little hard. His heavy chin was stubborn if not assertive. He still had the marks of the self-made man that he was, not yet refined to the ripe native genius which Europe took him for. He looked successful rather than superior."

Had Franklin been able to read Van Doren's description, he probably would have agreed. Perhaps he sat so often for so many artists later in his life to show that his genius *had* ripened, become visible. These works invariably display a man in the pose or attire of a scientist, but with bemusement on his lips and in his eyes indicating that he had not spent so much time at scientific pursuits as to have neglected life's more basic pleasures. He radiated contentment to such an extent that you want to shake him out of the frame, off the canvas, sit him down, and demand his secrets, or listen to his tales.

Despite this impression, Franklin almost always posed for artists grudgingly, with the single exception perhaps of the French sculptor Jean-Antoine Houdon. "He is of the first Reputation in his Profession," Franklin wrote of him in 1786, prior to sitting for a plaster bust, "and has a great Share of the Ambition I admire in an Artist, that of working as much for Fame as for Profit."

But by then Franklin had long since passed the point of being flattered by attention, having received so much of it for so many years. When his friend Thomas Digges asked for a portrait, telling

Franklin he was anticipating "the pleasure I shall receive in holding forever in my possession the likeness of the man to whom my Country owes the first & most extensive obligations," Franklin replied as civilly as he could: "I have at the request of friends sat so much and so often to painters and Statuaries, that I am perfectly sick of it. I know of nothing so tedious as sitting Hours in one fix'd Posture. I would nevertheless do it once more to oblige you if it was necessary, but there are already so many good Likenesses of the face, that if the best of them is copied it will probably be better than a new one, and the Body is only that of a lusty man which need not be drawn from Life: any Artist can add such a Body to the face."

We don't know whether Digges ever got his portrait or, if so, what manner of body supported the visage. But those who did receive an image of Franklin expressed in virtually all cases their delight. His friend Amelia Barry, for instance, had corresponded with him the previous year, letting him know that his picture, which she had obtained a few months earlier, was "a testimony of your condescending Friendship to me; and I shall in writing, enjoin my children to preserve and transmit this to their descendants, as a most sacred deposit, never to be parted with, till Virtue and Wisdom ceace to be objects of their pursuit."

Comments like this may have made all the hours of posing worthwhile — or at least tolerable — for Franklin, although he never admitted as much. Why endure all the tedium, though, if he didn't mean to elicit such reactions, not just the gratitude that Amelia Barry expressed but the promise that she would do her best to ensure the long life of the portrait?

George Washington spent more time looking at the back of an easel than any of the other founders. He had more requests for his portrait than the others, and responded with the modesty he revealed on most other occasions when people paid their respects to him.

One of the many requests came from the Marquis de Lafayette, the Frenchman who had served on Washington's staff in the Revolutionary War before returning to his homeland. There he joined with Franklin, Adams, and Jefferson to persuade the French to aid the American cause, thus serving the colonies both as soldier and statesman. But it was Washington whom Lafayette most admired, and whose picture he wanted to hang in a place of honor on his wall. He asked for one, and Washington wrote back with surprise: "Could I have conceived, that my Picture had been an object of your Wishes, or in the smallest degree worthy of your Attention, I should, while Mr. Peale was in the Camp at Valley forge, have got him to have taken the best Portrait of me he could, and presented it to you; but I really had not so good an opinion of my own worth, as to suppose that such a compliance would not have been considered as a greater instance of my Vanity, than a mean of your gratification."

The Mr. Peale to whom Washington refers is Charles Willson, of course, who had numbered Adams among his fans and had already painted Washington a few times and would paint him again. Peale was patriarch of the most distinguished family of artists in American history, having three wives and seventeen children, several of whom became painters themselves. None of them rivaled their father in composition or technique, but three established reputations of their own for their accomplishments in still life and portraiture. Peale's brother was also a painter, as were a nephew and four nieces.

In 1779, the year after Lafayette had asked for a picture of Washington, legislators in Pennsylvania decided that they wanted one as well and commissioned Peale to paint it. But they had something more in mind than just a show of the painter's gifts or the subject's appeal to their constituency. It was a source of inspiration they sought, one they could frame and display in the Pennsylvania statehouse. They wanted Peale to paint Washington so that when the picture was hung, it "may excite others to tread in the same glorious and disinterested steps which lead to public happiness and private honor." Peale went to work with just those goals in mind. It was how he would have rendered Washington even had he not known the legislators' desire. When he finished, Peale pronounced himself pleased with the results, and his subject felt the same.

Prior to a previous sitting for Peale, however, Washington had hesitated, afraid Peale was so good that he would reveal Washington's flaws rather than his attributes, would see through the dignity on the surface and find weakness and doubt beneath. "I am now contrary to all expectation under the hands of Mr. Peale," he wrote at the time, "but in so grave — so sullen a Mood — and now and then under the influence of Morpheus, when some critical strokes are making, that I fancy the skill of the Gentleman's Pencil will be put to it, in describing to the World what manner of Man I am."

Washington, of course, had nothing to fear from Peale, nor did he have reason to hesitate on those occasions when Gilbert Stuart painted him. Yet it was not always easy for Stuart, who recalled that sometimes "an apathy seemed to seize him [Washington], and a vacuity spread over his countenance most appalling to paint." At other times, Stuart found Washington too tense. He pleaded with the great man to relax. "Now, sir," he once said, "you must let me forget that you are General Washington and that I am Stuart the painter." Washington's reply, in the words of historian Gordon Woods, "chilled the air" with its unexpected arrogance. "Mr. Stuart need never feel the need of forgetting who he is," Washington said, "or who General Washington is."

Ultimately, though, the sessions were worth the effort for Stuart. "There were features in his face," the artist said of the general, "totally different from what I had observed in any other human being. All his features were indicative of the strongest passions; yet like Socrates his judgment and self-command made him appear a man of different cast in the eyes of the world."

Perhaps not all his features. There were those famous false teeth, a source of vexation not only to the wearer but to those who tried to reproduce him in a dignified manner. "The distortion of the mouth is minimal," writes biographer James Thomas Flexner about some of Stuart's better efforts. It was as hearty a compliment as Flexner could provide.

Another of the requests Washington received for an image came from General Friedrich-Christoph, count of Solms and Tecklenberg, a Saxon soldier and politician. He had long admired Washington from afar, and had converted one of the rooms of his castle to a portrait museum of his idols, among them Frederick the Great. Solms wanted to add Washington's picture to his collection, the only American he would so honor, and asked whether Washington would be kind enough to provide him one. He replied that he would: "I must entreat, my General," Washington wrote, "that you will accept my best acknowledgments for the favorable opinion you are pleased to express of my military character, as well as for your great politeness in proposing to introduce my likeness amongst your collection of heroes. . . . I have not delayed a moment therefore to comply with your wishes, but have employed a Gentleman to perform the work, who is thought on a former occasion to have taken a better likeness of me, than any other painter has done."

Washington tried to please both those who asked for a painting and those who turned them out, his snap at Stuart the rare exception. But like Adams and Franklin, he found the process tiresome, sometimes mind-numbing, and wondered whether he would ever get used to it. He did, but not easily or quickly. In 1785, with his reputation as a military leader established, a multitude of sittings behind him, and another multitude awaiting once he assumed the presidency, he wrote to his friend Francis Hopkinson, a signer of the Declaration of Independence. Hopkinson, too, wanted a portrait. Washington agreed, but let Hopkinson know that he complied with a certain lack of zest: "I am so hackneyed to the touches of the Painters pencil, that I am *now* altogether at their beck, and sit like patience on a Monument whilst they are delineating the lines of my face. It is a proof among many others, of what habit & custom can effect. At first

I was as impatient at the request, and as restive under the operation, as a Colt is of the Saddle — The next time, I submitted very reluctantly, but with less flouncing. Now, no dray moves more readily to the Thill,* than I do to the Painters Chair."

After several more years, near the end of his first term as president, Washington became less amenable to both artists and supplicants, referring to "the irksomeness of sitting, and the time I lose by it," and eventually reaching a point at which "I have resolved to sit no more for any of them and have adhered to it, except in instances where it has been requested by public bodies, or for a particular purpose (not of the Painters) and could not, without offence be refused."

He did, however, refuse to be sculpted in a manner suggesting royalty, rejecting a proposal that a statue be made of him wearing a toga, as if he were a Roman emperor. Hamilton had agreed to it; Washington would not. He preferred instead, as he put it in most understated fashion, "some little deviation in favor of the modern costume." The deviation was made, the notion of the toga rejected. Washington might have been fastidious in his attire, but he wasn't pompous, nor would he allow an artist to misrepresent his ideals in stone any more than he himself would misrepresent them in flesh and blood.

Like the rest of the Founding Fathers, Washington knew he would be remembered long after his time and insisted that he be remembered correctly. Perhaps in the final analysis, he and the other founders allowed themselves to be painted and molded as much as they did not just because they wanted to keep themselves alive forever, not just to indulge whatever vanity they possessed, but also out of a sense of historical justice. They had, after all, built the world's first instant nation: just add documents. They had demonstrated courage and genius, patience and perseverance, faith and finesse. The generations who came after them ought to know.

---

*A hitching device for draft animals.

Chapter 9
Myth

ON A FEW OCCASIONS, WASHINGTON TRIED to improve his image. It was biographers that he misled, however, not painters, and subsequent biographers had no trouble getting at the truth.

A few years after the Revolutionary War, David Humphreys, a Yale graduate who fancied himself a poet, approached Washington about writing the story of his life to date. Washington was reluctant, not wanting to call attention to himself in such a manner. But Humphreys pleaded, and Washington finally agreed, flattered by the young man's persistence. He could not, however, bring himself to tell Humphrey the truth about his early days as a soldier in the French and Indian War. Much time had passed, but his embarrassment about his conduct had not.

Initially, Washington had wanted to be a British officer. He did not mention that to Humphreys, even though there was no shame in such a goal for an American in the early 1750s, when colonies and Crown were one. Washington also neglected to mention that he had behaved poorly under his commanding officer, General John Forbes.

And he had badly mismanaged the defense of Fort Necessity, which he did relate to Humphreys, but in a version in which Washington was not the sole, or even primary, wrongdoer.

Having developed the habit of touching up the past, Washington continued with it after Humphreys finished his volume. He examined his voluminous correspondence over the years, especially his earliest writings, and didn't always like what he saw. He made some of his papers more legible when he thought there were too many erasures, and rewrote other pages entirely when he found too many deletions, excisions, or errors in grammar or spelling. He does not seem to have altered facts here, merely providing a tidier, more correct appearance. In the words of Joseph J. Ellis, he was "sanding down the rough edges of his pre-hero phase of development."

It was an understandable impulse, though unnecessary. Many years later an Episcopal priest named Mason Locke Weems wrote a biography in which he sanded and buffed the rough edges of Washington's life so much that they glowed with the radiance of a halo. Washington didn't have to deceive Weems, nor could he. He had died the year before the man put pen to paper. Weems — for what he believed to be the most socially and morally responsible of reasons — deceived his readers.

Parson Weems did not think of himself as a falsifier. Instead, like Horatio Alger early in the twentieth century, Weems had determined to write about a young man who had risen to pinnacles of achievement through pluck, daring, and stick-to-it-iveness. Like the Pennsylvania legislature, Weems wanted to showcase a hero who would inspire all who knew him to follow in his path. But Weems hoped to accomplish even more: the creation of a secular hero as saintly as Christ, the chronicle of his life becoming a sermon in the guise of an adventure tale. And who better for a subject than George Washington, about whom Weems could write in the same manner as he conducted his church services, with "long rhetorical flights, more emotional than logical, appealing to the heart rather than to the head."

Less than a month after Washington died, Weems sent a note to a friend, publisher Mathew Carey, informing him that he intended to tell Washington's story in an unconventional fashion. He did not want simply to relate the details of Washington's life, but "to show that his unparrelled rise & elevation were due to his Great Virtues," which were, among others, "1 his Veneration for the Diety or Religious Principles. 2 His Patriotism. 3d his Magninmity. 4 his Industry. 5 his Temperance & Sobriety. 6 his Justice, &c. &c. Thus I hold up his great Virtues . . . to the imitation of Our Youth."

At first, Carey had no interest in such a volume. But Weems went ahead with it anyhow, making other arrangements for the publication of the first few printings. The book turned out to be even more effusively written than his proposal. "To this day," he declared in the chapter on Washington's birth and education, "numbers of good Christians can hardly find faith to believe that Washington was, bona fide, *a Virginian! 'What! a buckskin!'* say they with a smile, *George Washington a buckskin! pshaw! impossible! he was certainly an European: So great a man could never have been born in America.*"

Later in the book, near the end of the Revolutionary War, Washington addresses his troops, trying to rally their spirits, to assure them that their countrymen appreciate their efforts, despite what seems at times a lack of support from officials of the national government: "As he spoke, his cheeks, naturally pale, were reddened over with virtue's pure vermillion; while his eyes of cerulean blue were kindled up with those indescribable fires which fancy lends to an angel orator, animating poor mortals to the sublime of god-like deeds. His words were not in vain. From lips of wisdom, and long tried love, like his, such counsel wrought as though an oracle had spoke."

It's enough to make a reader sniffle.

The first edition of *The Life and Memorable Actions of George Washington* by Mason Locke Weems appeared in 1800 and was an immediate success. It also proved to be an enduring success. After a quarter of a century, the book had gone through twenty-nine printings.

The parson became known as "the Father of the Father of His People."

But it was with the edition published in 1806 that the book passed from best-seller to literary legend, from lavishly embellished fact to fairy tale. In the 1806 edition, Weems added the story of George Washington and the cherry tree. It is the most enduring lie in American history.

> "When George," said she, "was about six years old, he was made the wealthy master of a *hatchet!* Of which, like most little boys, he was immoderately fond, and was constantly going about chopping every thing that came in his way. One day, in the garden, where he often amused himself hacking his mother's pea-sticks, he unluckily tried the edge of his hatchet on the body of a beautiful young English cherry-tree, which he barked so terribly, that I don't believe the tree ever got the better of it. The next morning the old Gentleman [Washington's father] finding out what had befallen his tree, which, by the by, was a great favourite, came into the house, and with much warmth asked for the mischievous author, declaring at the same time, that he would not have taken five guineas for his tree. Nobody could tell him any thing about it. Presently George and his hatchet made their appearance. *George*, said his father, *do you know who killed that beautiful little cherry-tree yonder in the garden?* This was a *tough question;* and George staggered under it a moment; but quickly recovered himself: and looking at his father, with the sweet face of youth brightened with the inexpressible charm of all-conquering truth, he bravely cried out, *'I can't tell a lie, Pa; you know I can't tell a lie. I did cut it with my hatchet.'* — *Run to my arms, you dearest boy,* cried his father in transports, *run to my arms; glad am I, George, that you killed my tree; for you have paid me for it a thousand fold. Such an act of heroism in my son, is more worth than a thousand trees, though blossomed with silver, and their fruits of purest gold."*

Weems was setting an example, he must have thought, not only to bolster the spirits of a young nation trying to survive and prosper but to resound through the centuries. The Bible had its parables; why should Weems's hagiography of Washington not make use of the same device? The purposes were identical: to direct the reader onto the paths of righteousness, not to impress him with, or bog him down in, the stultifying accuracy of detail.

It was also in the 1806 edition that Weems added another fiction, one that dwarfs the cherry tree in preposterousness, though it is not as well known now. At the time, however, it set tongues wagging as much as the anecdote of young George's honesty — and was questioned as little. After all, Weems's wife was a cousin of the late president, and the parson's church lay only a mile or two down the road from Mount Vernon. He was in a position to know the particulars of Washington family lore.

It seems, according to what was now called simply *The Life of Washington*, that young George had gone into the family's cabbage patch one day and found that some of the plants had sprung up not in rows but in letters of the alphabet, and the letters spelled out the name of George Washington! The boy was astonished, uncomprehending; how could such a thing be? Only one man would know. Washington ran to his father for an explanation.

Augustine Washington was oddly calm about the matter. He returned with his son to the patch, looked at the configuration of cabbages for a few moments, and then suggested it was mere chance. The boy would have none of it.

"Yes, Pa, but I did never see the little plants grow up so as to make *one single* letter of my name before. Now, how could they grow up so as to make *all* the letters of my name! and then standing one after another, to spell *my name* so *exactly!* — and all so neat and even too, at top and bottom!! O Pa, you must not say *chance* did all this. Indeed *somebody* did it; and I dare say now, Pa, *you* did do it just to scare *me*, because I am your little boy."

His father confessed. He *had* done it, he said, but for a reason that was well-intended if not altogether comprehensible.

> "I want, my son, to introduce you to your *true* father."
>
> "High, Pa, an't *you* my true father, that has loved me, and been so good to me always?"
>
> "Yes, George, I am your father as the world calls it: and I love you very dearly too. But yet with all my love for you, George, I am but a good-for-nothing sort of father in comparison of one you have."
>
> "Aye! I know well enough whom you mean, Pa. You mean God Almighty, don't you?"
>
> "Yes, my son, I mean him indeed. *He is* your true Father, George."

And on the story goes, with God's invisibility in earthly matters compared to Augustine Washington's invisibility in planting the cabbage seeds one day when the boy was otherwise engaged. "Perhaps it was at that moment," Weems wrote, after father and son had finished discussing the episode, "that the good Spirit of God ingrafted on [Washington's] heart that germ of *piety*, which filled his after life with so many of the precious fruits of *morality*."

Washington's later biographers doubted Weems, but could not bring themselves to ignore him. The lies about the cherry tree and the cabbage patch had become too deeply embedded in the culture. They were too good to be true, but that also made them too good to dismiss without mention. In 1887 Virginia F. Townsend wrote, "The story of the hatchet and the cherry sapling, whether true or not, is singularly characteristic. It shows the strong impression which the sensitive conscience of the child must have made on those around him. Nobody would ever have thought of relating such a story in connection with the boyhood of Napoleon Bonaparte."

In 1923 journalist O. W. Mosher Jr. defended the cherry tree fable in the *New York Times Magazine*. "Is it not fair to Weems to assume that he was merely recording an already well known incident? The story has high moral value for the youth of our nation. Why attempt to discredit it on insufficient grounds?"

In 1945, in the *Christian Science Monitor*, another journalist, Malcolm W. Bayley, criticized Weems's critics for failing to prove a negative. "While it has become customary for Washington biographers either to ignore the Cherry Tree story or to treat it as a tale without foundation — principally, perhaps, because no evidence has ever been unearthed to substantiate it — no one of them, including several who made a study of the life of the Rev. Mason Locke Weems of Virginia, has ever proved that the industrious parson made up the story out of whole cloth."

And as late as 1954, Bella Koral, author of a children's book about Washington, upheld Weems's fables on the grounds of extreme repetition. "Stories about George Washington as a boy," she stated, "have been retold so often through the years that even though we're not sure they really did happen, they have become a part of the story of America. And they do tell us something of the kind of boy he was."

Others were not so accepting. Albert J. Beveridge, a senator from Indiana at the turn of the twentieth century and author of a four-volume biography of John Marshall, chief justice under Jefferson, tore into Weems for his "grotesque and imaginary stories." These did not make Washington the Christian exemplar that Weems intended, Beveridge believed, but "an impossible and intolerable prig." Roscoe Thayer, whose biography of Washington appeared in 1922, blasted Weems's "pernicious drivel," his "errors and absurdities." And Rupert Hughes, who also wrote a biography of Washington in the 1920s, refers to a scarcity of information about the subject's early life, a "gap that Parson Weems filled up with such slush of plagiarism and piety."

Ultimately, though, Weems got exactly what he wanted. Through all of the nineteenth century and the early part of the twentieth, he made Washington into a figure whose courage, rectitude, and decency could not be questioned and whose example shone with celestial radiance. Washington might not have become more famous as a result, but — even better, as far as Weems was concerned — he became more deserving of the kind of fame that would last and enlighten forever. The parson's failures as a biographer were his triumphs as a moralist.

And he triumphed again a few years later when he wrote *The Life of Benjamin Franklin; With Many Choice Anecdotes and Admirable Sayings of This Great Man Never Before Published by Any of His Biographers.* The book teems with incidents that cannot be verified and dialogue that neither Weems nor any other human being could possibly have overheard.

Weems's biography of Franklin, as you might imagine, also brims with effusions, from the first page . . .

> As to his physiognomy, there was in it such an air of wisdom and philanthropy, and consequently such an expression of majesty and sweetness, as charms, even in the commonest pictures of him.

. . . to the barely comprehensible last page, which referred to him as a man whose name

> lives among the clouds of heaven. The lightnings, in their dreadful courses, bow to the genius of Franklin. His magic rods, pointed to the skies, still watch the irruption of the FIERY METEORS. They seize them by their hissing heads as they dart forth, from the dark chambers of the thunders; and cradled infants, half waked by the sudden glare, are seen to curl the cherub smile hard by the spot where the dismal bolts had fallen.

As far as anyone knows, John Adams did not take issue with either of Weems's fanciful biographies, speaking against them neither publicly nor privately. Many years earlier, when Weems was a child, Adams had written: "Writers who procure Reputation by flattering human

Nature, tell us that Mankind grows wiser and wiser: whether they lie, or speak the Truth, I know I like it, better and better."

And midway through the next century, in a conversation with a friend about George Washington, Abraham Lincoln expressed a similar view. "It makes human nature better to believe that one human being was perfect, that human perfection is possible."

William Wirt had a similar sentiment in mind when he produced his *Sketches of the Life and Character of Patrick Henry*. According to Henry biographer Robert Douthat Meade, writing in the mid-twentieth century, "Wirt seems to have adopted, not too wisely at times, the method of Parson Weems . . . [who] not satisfied with Washington's authentic greatness, did not hesitate to add stories about him of the most doubtful accuracy." Meade goes on: "Like Weems, Wirt indulged in romanticizing and painted vivid contrasts without always considering the final effects of his efforts. Somehow it would not do to give Henry credit for a normal upbringing, for all the results of tutoring by his learned father. Genius had to spring forth full blown."

Or, as Wirt himself put it in the book, Henry "was, indeed, a mere child of nature, and nature seems to have been too proud and too jealous of her work, to permit it to be touched by the hand of art."

Like the Weems biography of Washington, Wirt's book, published in 1817, became a best-seller, went through a number of printings, and influenced other biographers for generations to come — although not immediately and not as often. More than half a century passed before the next account of Patrick Henry's life appeared.

Here the similarities end, though. Weems wanted to create a role model for children, a figure whose every thought and deed were based firmly in Christian precepts. Wirt, a prominent lawyer who later served as attorney general under James Monroe and John Quincy Adams, intended something more grand. He wanted to pioneer a literary tradition in a country so new that it scarcely had any authors, much less a national oeuvre. In 1817, James Fenimore Cooper had not written the first of his *Leatherstocking Tales*. Washington Irving had turned out little more than a comic history of New York. Nathaniel Hawthorne was thirteen. Herman Melville would not be born for another two years, and Mark Twain's *father* was still in his teens.

Wirt wanted to be one of America's first great men of letters and, like Weems, thought his chances would be better if he chose a protagonist from real life, someone his fellow citizens already knew, yet did not know so well that fictionalizing him from time to time was out of the question. Wirt "genuinely admired his subject," writes Patrick Henry scholar James M. Elson, "who was in so many ways like himself; and, on a practical level, he knew very well that fame and fortune would certainly not come his way by writing a critical biography of the Voice of the Revolution."

And so it was that Wirt, at least in places, described his subject in laudatory terms. "His was a spirit fitted to raise the whirlwind, as well as to ride in and direct it. His was that comprehensive view, that unerring prescience, that perfect command over the actions of men, which qualified him not merely to guide, but almost to create the destinies of nations." Yet shortly after Wirt had settled on his project, he also began complaining about it. The biography quickly turned into an "irksome labor," he found, in part because it demanded too much time. As he stated in his preface, in the third person, Wirt "is a practicing lawyer; and the courts which he attends, keep him perpetually and exclusively occupied in that attendance through ten months of the year; nor does the summer recess of two months afford a remission from professional labor."

Wirt also noted in his preface that the materials he was able to assemble about his subject's life were "scanty and meager, and utterly disproportionate in the great fame of Mr. Henry."

It was a problem for Wirt — but also a windfall. After all, the fewer the facts, the greater the license for creativity. Perhaps the dearth of information about Henry — which is one of the reasons there are not more biographies of him — gave Wirt the opportunity he had wanted all along to indulge his fancies, to create a hero more in line with his literary sensibilities than the historical record. He admits as much when he says he will plug up the gaps in the record with "all the plaster of Paris" he can mix together.

But in this case there was no sanding down of rough edges. Perhaps if Henry were flawed, more a creature of flesh and blood than Weems's Washington, Wirt's book would have a verisimilitude lacking in the other volume and would therefore be more likely to qualify as literature and withstand the ages.

Wirt asked Thomas Jefferson to help him mix his plaster of Paris. It was, on the surface, the strangest of choices. Jefferson found Patrick Henry inept, ruthless, and patriotically fervid.

In fact, Jefferson and Henry were destined for an uncongenial relationship from the outset. For one, they were men of different natures, Jefferson delicate in his sensibilities, content in solitude, Henry more rough-and-tumble, outgoing, and impassioned. For another, Jefferson was born into a higher caste of Virginia society and may have resented Henry's climb to a degree of acclaim to which his lineage did not seem to entitle him. For yet another, when the Virginia legislature voted for its inquiry into Jefferson's conduct as the colony's wartime governor, Henry supported the motion. He did so, he claimed, not out of any animosity or the conviction that Jefferson had acted improperly, but because he believed the legislature was entitled to any information the governor could provide. Jefferson neither believed Henry nor forgave him, and found an opportunity to get even when Wirt interviewed him for the biography.

To begin with, Jefferson impugned Henry's education, and Wirt not only accepted the judgment but repeated it several times in his book.

I cannot learn that [Henry] gave, in his youth, any evidence of that precocity which sometimes distinguishes uncommon genius. His companions recollect no instance of premature wit, no striking sentiment, no remarkable beauty or strength of expression. . . . His person is represented as having been coarse, his manners uncommonly awkward, his dress slovenly, his conversation very plain, his aversion to study invincible, and his faculties almost entirely benumbed by indolence. No persuasion could bring him either to read or to work.

The truth was that Henry read diligently and worked hard. He might not have mastered the law when he started out, but he improved as the years went on. He had also studied the classics as a young man, kept up with his reading as an adult, and proved himself in a number of public forums.

Jefferson also denounced Henry's character to Wirt, even though, with the exception of the Parson's Cause, and some possibly questionable land deals in his later years, Henry behaved honorably throughout his career. And about one of the land deals Wirt admitted that there was "no law of the state" forbidding it; about another, "he was blamed . . . for having availed himself of the existing laws of the state." Questionable, perhaps, but not criminal.

Jefferson charged Henry with lacking fortitude, but here too the accusation falls flat. There is no evidence that Henry ever acted timidly or shirked his duty in any matter of consequence. He certainly didn't hesitate to make known his opposition to the British as war drew closer, and his speeches before various legislative assemblies, some of them previously cited, were not those of a pusillanimous man.

Jefferson also told Wirt that Henry had had virtually no role in writing a series of resolutions passed by the Virginia Assembly that expressed outrage with the Stamp Act — the most controversial set of taxes ever imposed on the colonies by Parliament. In fact, Henry collaborated with three of his fellow Virginia legislators in composing every one of the resolutions. Wirt included all of Jefferson's views in his biography, presenting them as facts, as he did with other fallacious characterizations from other sources. When he ran short on those, he made up a few of his own.

And so there is in the *Sketches of the Life and Character of Patrick Henry*, if not an abundance of truth, at least a kind of balance — passages that make his subject seem gifted, especially in the courtroom, where his eloquence "was so unexampled, so unexpected, so instantaneous, and so transcendent in its character, that it had, to the people, very much the appearance of supernatural inspiration." Those who heard him try a case "considered him as bringing his credentials directly from heaven, and owing no part of his greatness to human institutions."

Yet other passages dismiss Henry as unconscionably inept in the courtroom, "so little acquainted with the fundamental principles of his profession, and so little skilled in that system of artificial reason on which the common law is built, as not to be able to see the remote bearings of the reported cases."

Henry also seems to be the kind of person who would chop down an entire orchard of cherry trees and refuse to accept the blame. Not to mention greedy. "In his accumulation [of wealth]," Wirt wrote, "he was charged with wringing from the hands of his clients, and more particularly those of the criminals he defended, fees rather too exorbitant." Notice, however, that Wirt does not tell us who made the charges. Someone trustworthy? A foe who would say anything to tarnish Henry's reputation?

And then, almost dizzyingly, Wirt refers to Henry as a man whose "morals were strict. As a husband, a father, a master, he had no superior. He was kind and hospitable to the stranger, and most friendly and accommodating to his neighbours. In his dealings with the world, he was faithful in his promise, and punctual in his contracts, to the utmost of his power. "

These conflicting images illuminate the differences between Weems and Wirt, the latter believing that his alternating views of his subject resulted in a more interesting story than Weems's panegyric of Washington. Whereas the Weems biography reads like a collection of homilies spiced with anecdotes, the Wirt, although more admiring of its subject than not, has at its center an imperfect protagonist, which gives the book the emotional complexity of good fiction.

Some years later, if Wirt read Cooper's *The Pioneers*, the first of his Leatherstocking Tales, he might well have believed that Cooper got the idea for his son of the wilderness, Natty Bumppo, at least in part from Wirt's rendering of Patrick Henry.

Ironically, despite his many contributions to Wirt's effort, Jefferson called it "a poor book written in bad taste." Of course, Jefferson, as much as Wirt, must take the blame for some of the imperfections.

The ultimate verdict on the *Sketches*, though, belongs to Henry's family, who believed that the author created a man for the ages, an essentially admirable figure whose lapses give the impression of a true-to-life creature of flesh and blood, in contrast to Weems's Washington, whose impossibly virtuous behavior makes him seem almost a fairy-tale figure. After all, Henry's grandson, who compiled Henry's letters and speeches and a biography into a three-volume set of inestimable value to historians, was christened by his parents William Wirt Henry.

Weems and Wirt were exceptions. Other early biographers of the Founding Fathers did not go to such extremes of falsification to suit their purposes. But falsify they did from time to time. They exaggerated, ignored, simplified, and recontextualized to present a more favorable view of their idols and a more negative one of their villains. Virtually all the biographies and biographical fragments that appeared in the first century after the deaths of the founders were rave reviews of the lives they led — seldom mixed and never pans. This holds for accounts of Franklin by James Parton, J. B. McMaster, and J. T. Morse; accounts of Hamilton by Samuel W. McCall, Chard Powers Smith, William Graham Sumner, and Charles A. Shriner;

accounts of Jefferson by B. L. Rayner, Gilbert Chinard, and Albert J. Nock; accounts of John Adams by Timothy Pickering and Winslow Watson; the account of Sam Adams by W. V. Wells; and accounts of John Hancock by John R. Musick and Stephen Higginson — to name a few.

The Declaration of Independence and the Constitution put forth the ideals for the new nation; the early biographies of the founders personified those ideals. As the founders strove for fame in their lifetimes, each in his own way, biographers joined with painters and sculptors to preserve that fame, even to enlarge it. All who reproduced the images of the Founding Fathers, verbally or pictorially, feared that if they disappointed their subjects, they would also disappoint posterity.

Part III

The Last Days of Famous Men

Chapter 10
A Simple Epitaph

AS TIME RAN OUT ON BENJAMIN FRANKLIN, he began to think more about his soul than his reputation. He had not been particularly devout as a younger man. Genial to all faiths, committed to none, he never showed much interest in asking such questions as whether there was life after death and, if so, what forms it might take. Science, civic improvement, and diplomacy had always engaged him more. His insistence in letters to friends, as he grew old, that he believed in heaven, or something like it, may have been as much an effort to persuade himself as it was an actual statement of his views. "I look upon death to be as necessary to our constitution as sleep," he concluded one of those letters. "We shall rise refreshed in the morning."

But did he really think so? The phrase sounds more rehearsed than heartfelt, like something from *Poor Richard's Almanac* rather than Ben Franklin's well of innermost convictions.

Later, contemplating the matter more carefully, with a different metaphor, he compared the workings of nature, which he regarded as an example of almost perfect efficiency, to the Almighty's plan for the human beings He had created. "When I see nothing annihilated," he said, "and not even a drop of water wasted, I cannot suspect the annihilation of souls, or believe that [God] will suffer the daily waste of millions of minds ready made that now exist, and put himself to the continual trouble of making new ones." Some historians believe he is admitting the possibility of reincarnation here, as in the previously cited excerpt — although once again the writing seems more clever than sincere, more wishful than assured.

What is important, though, is that Franklin was addressing the subject of immortality, something he had done rarely in the past. He had no new experiments to conduct as an old man, no new suggestions for a better Philadelphia, no negotiating tables in foreign capitals awaiting his presence. As a man's life comes to an end, the number of topics that interest him, as well as the number of people who depend on him, diminishes. The year that Franklin died, at age eighty-four, he received a letter asking for his thoughts on religion from Ezra Stiles, a friend who had been a librarian, minister, anthropologist, and president of Yale University. Franklin was not in the best of health at the time, but Stiles's question surprised him. As simple and basic as it was, no one had ever asked him before — at least no one of Stiles's stature, who would expect a thoughtful response. Franklin was taken aback. What exactly *did* he think of religion, the whole panoply of views and beliefs that constituted a faith, now that the end was in sight for him?

"Here is my creed," he wrote after much contemplation. "I believe in one God, creator of the universe. That he governs it by his providence. That he ought to be worshipped. That the most acceptable service we render to him is doing good to his other children. That the soul of man is immortal, and will be treated with justice in another life, respecting its conduct in this. These I take to be the fundamental principles of all sound religion, and I regard them as you do in whatever sect I meet with them."

As for Jesus, Franklin commended his moral teachings and the lengths to which he went to promote them. After all, He had served as one of Franklin's two main role models as a young man. But was Jesus the son of God, as Christianity taught? Franklin didn't know. He admitted, however, that "it is a question I do not dogmatize upon, having never studied it, and I think it needless to busy myself with it now, when I expect soon an opportunity of knowing the truth with less trouble." For this reason, Franklin pleaded with Stiles not to publish his letter or show it to mutual acquaintances, not wanting to offend those who accepted Jesus's divinity.

After more ruminating, Franklin concluded his letter as follows: "I shall only add, respecting myself, that, having experienced the goodness of that Being in conducting me prosperously through a long life, I have no doubt of its continuance in the next, though without the smallest conceit of meriting such goodness."

Having achieved all the notice he could during his long life, Franklin was hoping now to be noticed by the Almighty, to Whom he would neither demonstrate nor admit the slightest trace of vanity.

Franklin died a month later, on April 17, 1790. To the ordinary men and women of America, from whose ranks he had risen and in which, in some ways, he still resided, it was a national tragedy, however expected. In Philadelphia, shops closed, government offices closed, no business of any sort was transacted. There had been so much noise, so much commotion, when Franklin returned from France in 1785 — the cannons firing, the huzzahs from those awaiting him. Now, according to Carl Van Doren, "The bells were muffled and tolled. The flags on the ships in the harbour hung at half-mast." An estimated 20,000 people watched Franklin's funeral procession, the largest crowd that had ever assembled in the city and also the most eerily silent. At the procession's end, as if assuming a position of uncertainty, came Philadelphia's men of the cloth. Some think that every preacher in town showed up to march behind Franklin's remains. Certainly every church was represented, a few by more than one cleric. They all wanted to claim him as their own. They wanted to do what they could to get his afterlife off to a proper start.

The federal government did surprisingly little. At the urging of James Madison, the House of Representatives paid tribute to Franklin, calling on its members to wear black for a month. The motion passed unanimously, but a similar motion failed in the Senate, where legislators were not so much snubbing the deceased as they were acceding to the whims of their presiding officer, the vice president of the United States, who saw no reason to change his opinion of Franklin just because he had died. The senators believed that John Adams would have vetoed, or attempted to veto, any effort by their body to express either condolences or appreciation for Franklin. They did not want to dishonor his memory by dragging it through such controversial circumstances. Adams said nothing.

The president did not act either, although for different reasons. As explained by Jefferson, then secretary of state, "I proposed to General Washington that the executive department should wear mourning; he declined it, because he said he would not know where to draw the line if he once began that ceremony. . . . I told him that the world had drawn so broad a line between him and Dr. Franklin, on the one side, and the residue of mankind, on the other, that we might wear mourning for them, and the question still remain new and undecided as to all others. He thought it best, however, to avoid it."

In France, no such reservations existed. The country grieved as it had never grieved before, not even for its own philosophers, Voltaire and Rousseau, both of whom had died a few years before. And it grieved as it has never grieved since for a foreigner, with the possible exception of President Kennedy almost two centuries later.

The National Assembly sent a message of condolence to officials in the United States, but almost apologetically, admitting that there was no way it could adequately convey the depth of its sorrow. It declared three days of official mourning, but unofficial mourning lasted much longer and among more people, men and women from all walks of life. Newspapers wrote editorials lamenting Franklin's death every day for weeks, as if issuing a paean for each of his achievements. Clergymen wrote eulogies and delivered them Sunday after Sunday. Private citizens came up with their own eulogies and either read or improvised them to one another at gatherings both formal and informal. A pall hung over the salons where once Franklin had once held forth. Some of them didn't even bother to assemble for a while, their members having no heart for conviviality. People thought back fondly to the days Franklin had spent among them. They reread his writings or bought them for the first time. They remembered him, they studied him, they looked at the numerous likenesses of him they had kept as personal treasures, they saluted all that he had been. In a way — Franklin would have been amused if not altogether pleased by the word — they worshipped him.

More than sixty years earlier, at the age of twenty-eight and as a kind of jest, Franklin had written an epitaph for himself. The style was typical, as were the humor and self-confidence. It is also worth noting that the words foreshadow Franklin's later belief in — or hope for — some form of eternal life.

> The body of
> B. Franklin, Printer;
> (Like the cover of an old book,
> Its contents worn out,
> And stripped of its lettering and gilding)
> Lies here, food for worms.
> But the work shall not be lost:
> For it will, (as he believed) appear once more,
> In a new and more elegant edition,
> Revised and corrected
> By the author.

When the time finally came for Franklin to write his last words, he had long since forgotten the above. He instead wrote the few words that appear on his gravestone, on a plot he shares with his wife. It reads:

BENJAMIN
     And   } FRANKLIN
DEBORAH
1790

He needed nothing more elaborate to call himself to the everlasting attention of Americans, Frenchmen, and, eventually, citizens from all over the world.

Chapter 11
The Tombstone at Red Hill

I N 1794, AFTER HE HAD RETIRED from government service, Patrick Henry retired again, this time from what might have been the most successful law practice in Virginia, one that both Jefferson and his long-ago examiners would have thought beyond his abilities. But he was fifty-eight years old now and felt older. He had had enough of the lawyer's life: too much study, too many trials, too little time for other interests. So he closed his office and bought an estate called Red Hill, near Appomattox, on more than 2,900 acres of fertile, picturesque farmland overlooking the Staunton River Valley. The property included a small house, a barn, and several outbuildings. Henry grew tobacco, corn, and rye — the last not a profitable crop in its natural state but a windfall when used to make whiskey. He converted one of the outbuildings into a distillery and reaped and sipped the profits.

Red Hill was an Eden to him. He swore he would never leave. He came very close to keeping his word.

Unlike Washington and Jefferson, who had held their properties for many years, Henry came late to landowning on a grand scale, and he delighted in it, with every day proving to be not only a challenge but a learning experience. He spent the last five years of his life managing his estate, enjoying the views, and turning down one offer after another to return to a prominent position in national affairs, which sometimes occupied more of his time than his other duties.

Shortly after settling into Red Hill, he was appointed to a seat in the Senate. Then President Washington asked him to serve as minister to Spain, and a year or so later suggested the same post in France. Washington also wanted him to be as secretary of state, and after that chief justice. President Adams named Henry a special envoy to France, with the Senate voting overwhelmingly to confirm before Henry even responded. On several occasions, he was asked to declare himself a candidate for the presidency and on other occasions for vice president. In addition to which, after already having served five terms as governor of Virginia, he was elected to a sixth.

To all of these offices, every one of them, he said no. He did not want the exertion, he had no desire for the attention. "I have long learned the little value to be placed on popularity," he wrote to his daughter in 1796, "acquired by any way other than virtue." He could be as virtuous at Red Hill as anywhere else.

But in 1799, already in the grip of his last illness, Henry acceded to another plea from Washington, who himself would die before the year was out. Washington wanted Henry to run for a seat in the Virginia House of Delegates, a governing body close to Henry's heart and home. It was a gesture more than anything else. Washington didn't expect Henry to serve a full term — perhaps not even to survive long enough to be sworn in.

But the House of Delegates had become a breeding ground of confusion and contentiousness. Its members, dividing into special interest groups, spent more time arguing over local matters and such national concerns as the Alien and Sedition Acts than they did legislating. As a result, the state's business wasn't getting done. Washington believed that if Henry made himself available for a seat in the House of Delegates, those already seated would be shamed into more suitable behavior, chastened both by Henry's eminence and his interest in joining their ranks. In other words, Washington assumed, Henry would act as a powerful force for reform even if he never opened his mouth.

But open it he did, giving one last speech to announce his candidacy for the office. It was early March, on the green in the center of Charlottesville. No one who heard Henry that day would ever forget it.

He departed from Red Hill on a Sunday, arriving in Charlottesville on Monday morning and making his way immediately, although not energetically, to the courthouse. He took a place on the front porch, after tenuously climbing the steps. In the words of an eyewitness:

> He was very infirm, and seated in a chair conversing with some friends who were pouring in from all the surrounding country to hear him. At length he arose with difficulty, and stood, somewhat bowed with age and weakness. His face was almost colorless. His countenance was careworn, and when he commenced his exordium, his voice was slightly cracked and tremulous. But in a few moments a wonderful transformation of the whole man occurred, as he warmed with his theme. He stood erect: his eyes beamed with a light that was almost supernatural; his features glowed with the hue and fire of youth; and his voice rang clear and melodious.

"If I am asked what is to be done when a people feel themselves intolerably oppressed," Henry said, "my answer is ready: *Overturn the government.*" Such a step should always be a last resort, he said, whether the government in question was a state, to which he referred in this case, or the Crown, as it had been many years earlier. In the meantime, he said, "Let us trust God and our better judgment to set us right hereafter. United we stand, divided we fall. Let us not split into factions which must destroy that union upon which our existence hangs. Let us preserve our strength for the French, the English, the Germans, or in whoever else shall dare invade our territory, and not exhaust it in civil commotions and intestine wars."

When he finished, the crowd roared in approval, realizing they would never hear these sentiments expressed again — not in that language, not in those tones, not by this man. Henry acknowledged the accolades with a few bows and waves, and then those closest to him on the courthouse porch escorted him inside to rest. Henry dropped heavily into a chair. Said one of his companions, commenting both on the oration and the man who had delivered it, "The sun has set in all its glory."

But Henry's most remarkable utterance of the day had come an hour or two before that. It was shorter, more improvised, and spoken so softly that only a handful of people heard it.

When he arrived in Charlottesville that morning, a crowd gathered to welcome him and follow him to the courthouse. They patted him on the back, wished him well in his address, hung on whatever words he had the strength to utter in response — fans gathering around a celebrity then just as they do today. They were delighted that he had come to rescue the House of Delegates.

From afar, a Baptist minister watched the scene and found the adulation more than he could bear. He approached the old man and his entourage with fire in his eyes, stopping a few feet away.

"Mr. Henry is not a god!" he shouted, trying to dissuade his fellow citizens from treating him as one. A hush came over them instantly. They turned to Henry, wondering how he would react. At first he said nothing. Then, looking at the minister, squinting to bring him into focus, he took a few steps in his direction. The crowd parted to let him proceed.

"No, indeed, my friend," he said to the clergyman. "I am but a poor worm of the dust — as fleeting and unsubstantial as a shadow of the cloud that flies over yon fields, and is remembered no more."

The minister made no reply. Henry bowed to him slightly. The crowd remained silent. After a few moments, Henry continued his trek to the courthouse, his fellow Virginians still accompanying him but now at a slight distance. The preacher held his ground. The mood of the day had changed dramatically.

Just as the speech from the courthouse porch was Henry's last significant public utterance, so was his reply to the minister his last public profession of modesty. "No man ever vaunted less of his achievements than Mr. Henry," said his son-in-law, Spencer Roane:

> As for *boasting*, he was an entire stranger to it; unless it be that in his latter days he seemed proud of the goodness of his lands, and, I believe, wished to be thought wealthy. It is my opinion that he was better pleased to be flattered as to his wealth than as to his great talents. This I have accounted for by reflecting that he had long been under narrow and difficult circumstances as to property, from which he was at length happily relieved, whereas there never was a time when his talents had not shone conspicuous, tho' he always seemed unconscious of them.

Others were not unconscious of them, however, and believed that his talents would be remembered long after he had passed away. Among them was John Adams who stated that, because of his work on the Stamp Act Resolutions, Henry would "have the glory with posterity of beginning and concluding this great revolution." Henry was pleased with the compliment but went no further in acknowledging it than to repeat his previously expressed hope "that posterity should pronounce us [Henry and John and Sam Adams] descended from the same stock."

When Henry died on June 6, 1799, at the age of sixty-three, his fellow Virginian Edmund Randolph, who served Washington both as attorney general and, after Jefferson's resignation, as secretary of state, was among the first to offer a valedictory: Henry was without peer as a defender of liberty, Randolph affirmed, not only in the United

States but in the entire hemisphere. A Virginia newspaper that supported Henry's views mourned him as no newspaper today would mourn a public figure: "Farewell, first-rate patriot, farewell! As long as our rivers flow, or mountains stand — so long will your excellence and worth be the theme of homage and endearment, and Virginia, bearing in mind her loss, will say to rising generations, imitate my *HENRY*."

Such effusiveness would have embarrassed Henry. Then again, maybe not. He lived at a time when renown, if properly achieved, was considered a virtue, and no matter how many times he demonstrated his humility and dismissed public notice, no matter how little he seemed to care about leaving behind a portrait or bust for future generations to contemplate, no matter how privately he tended to his public business, he was a man of his era, still the man who had thrown decency aside for the sake of ambition in the trial of Reverend James Maury, however much he might have changed in the thirty-six years that followed. But he had long since become a member of the club of patriots who made the American revolution. His tombstone at Red Hill admitted Henry's private feelings about public notice:

To the memory of Patrick Henry

Born May 29, 1736.

Died June 6, 1799.

His fame his best epitaph.

Chapter 12
An Early Death

*G*IVEN THE TEMPERATURE at which Alexander Hamilton's ambition burned, we know he wanted his name to live forever. Given the unprecedented fiscal reforms he enacted for the United States, we know he wanted his deeds to live forever. Given his belief in reforms that were not enacted, we know he wanted future lawmakers to bring them up again and attest to their wisdom by approving them, whether or not he was around to soak in the approval. That is precisely what has happened.

More than any other founder, Hamilton left a legacy in the workings of the federal government today — the big, centralized government he so strongly favored, although its current size might have appalled even him. He reformed the U.S. Customs Service. He advocated a national debt, which over the years has grown larger than he would have approved. He encouraged foreign trade for the good of the U.S. economy. He argued for creation of the Federal Reserve System, which was not established until 1914. Our legislative and executive branches are still following his blueprints for the nation.

Washington thought Hamilton would live on simply because of his authorship of the Federalist Papers, and told him so in 1788. "When the transient circumstances and fugitive performances which attended this Crisis [over the interpretation of the Constitution] shall have disappeared, That Work will merit the Notice of Posterity, because in it are candidly and ably discussed the principles of freedom and the topics of government, which will be always interesting to mankind so long as they shall be connected in Civil Society."

But Alexander Hamilton died young. He was forty-nine when Aaron Burr killed him, and he had not left behind any thoughts about the role he hoped to play in the reminiscences of his countrymen and their descendants. Nor was he able to turn his thoughts in that direction in his final hours. He survived little more than a day after having been shot but was in such pain that his thoughts were muddled, and most of them turned to his wife and children. He thought about what had already become of his oldest son Philip, who had himself died in a duel a few years earlier, leaving him bereft. Why the elder Hamilton would then subject himself to the same kind of confrontation is a question that cannot be answered. Perhaps he believed that he was as invincible as his ideas.

Hamilton also thought about his Maker as he approached their meeting. "I have a tender reliance on the mercy of the Almighty," he said in his final hours, "through the merits of the Lord Jesus Christ." And the Lord, he was certain, knew Hamilton's shortcomings. "I am a sinner," he said to a friend who was also an Episcopal clergyman. "I look to His mercy." Two friends of long standing, both men of the cloth, attended Hamilton as the life ebbed out of him, and he begged them both to give him holy communion. Initially, albeit reluctantly, they refused; Hamilton had received his mortal wounds in a duel, a practice of which the church disapproved. At the last minute, though, one of the men, the Reverend Benjamin Moore, changed his mind and administered the sacrament. Dueling is a "barbarous custom," Moore declared, but Alexander Hamilton was a special case.

★   ★   ★

History records a mixed verdict on Hamilton. To some he was "the creator of American capitalism," which meant that he favored the rich at the expense of the poor, the investor at the expense of the laborer. Hamilton's brand of economics, said his critics, heartlessly reflected his own personal greed, his quest for wealth and power at the expense of others.

He would not have been surprised to know that Thomas Jefferson did not grieve over his departure. Jefferson had long believed that Hamilton's life "from the moment at which history can stoop to notice him, is a tissue of machinations against the liberty of the country which has not only received and given him bread, but heaped its honors on his head." Nor would Hamilton have been surprised to know that John Adams did not mourn his passing, that he barely acknowledged it at the time and continued to berate him after he had been dead several years. "Vice, folly, and villainy," Adams wrote in his autobiography, "are not to be forgotten because the guilty wretch repented in his dying moments."

Those who have written about Hamilton more recently have been kinder. To Ron Chernow, he was "an exuberant genius," to Willard Sterne Randall a man whose "reputation for honesty" was well deserved, and to Richard Brookhiser the possessor of "an all-pervading ardor" who "loved his ideas, his work, and his friends." Such conclusions would have cheered Hamilton, though not the time it took biographers to reach them.

And Hamilton would have been cheered by the efforts of his wife not only to preserve her late husband's name but to exalt it, to gain respect for it, by trying to strike from the record that long-ago dalliance of his. But she was not interested in a biography, not even the kind that a Parson Weems might have produced. Instead, she wanted her husband to speak for himself.

She began by hiring a number of assistants, perhaps as many as thirty, to go through her husband's papers and make some sense of them: sort them according to date, organize them according to topic, assemble the evidence that he was among the greatest Americans of his era and deserved to be recalled reverently ever after. The papers were voluminous: pamphlets and articles that he wrote about politics, economics, trade, and other subjects; pamphlets and articles about him; his notes on legislation; letters to and from Washington and others.

Eliza intended a massive and laudatory chronicle of Hamilton's life and times: several volumes, many pounds, thousands of pages — the arc of a relatively short but vastly accomplished life. The work was compiled, one of her sons as the editor, but she didn't live to see it. She died in 1854, seven years before John Church Hamilton's edition of *The Works of Alexander Hamilton: Comprising His Correspondence and His Political and Official Writings, Exclusive of the Federalist, Civil, and Military* appeared.

Its seven volumes begin with a letter that twelve-year-old Alexander wrote to his good friend from Nevis, Ned Stevens, the letter cited earlier in which he confesses that his "ambition is prevalent," and his condition "grovelling." The final volume concludes with a variety of speculations, notably about the political prospects of John Lansing, a long-time jurist, and soon-to-be-duelist Aaron Burr. Hamilton is quoted as saying he believed that Burr was the more likely of the two to hold high national office one day, making a brief but rueful comment about "the son of President Burr."

By the time John Church Hamilton's books appeared, Alexander Hamilton's tombstone had been standing in the graveyard of Trinity Church in New York for more than half a century, already showing the effects of the years. The inscription had worn down, and the grass had grown tall around the stone.

The inscription, which gives Hamilton's age incorrectly, was probably composed by one or more of the Trinity clergy, who, like Hamilton's family, had no doubt about the place of the man in the history of his nation.

To the memory of
ALEXANDER HAMILTON
The Corporation of Trinity Church Has erected this
Monument
In Testimony of their Respect
For
The PATRIOT of incorruptible INTEGRITY,
The SOLDIER of approved VALOUR,
The STATESMAN of consummate WISDOM;
Whose TALENTS and VIRTUES will be admired
By
Grateful Posterity
Long after this MARBLE shall have mouldered into DUST.
He died July 12th, 1804, Aged 47.

Hamilton couldn't have said it better himself.

Chapter 13
The Tourist Attraction

O N MARCH 15, 1797, A COACH CARRYING GEORGE WASHINGTON
and his family rattled up the familiar driveway of a familiar
house that Washington called "my long forsaken residence." The
coach stopped at the front door, and he planted his feet on his own
soil again, his eyes sweeping the terrain, his lips curving into a smile.
Like Henry, he swore he would never depart — not for any significant time, not for any significant reason.

But Washington knew that age as much as inclination would
keep him in place. He had already outlived the average man of his
era by a decade, and sometimes, like Henry, he felt every day of the
difference. His bones ached more than they used to, he was more
prone to illness, less likely to recover quickly. He wondered how
many days he had left. The smile on his return must have been a
wistful one.

He had handed over the presidency to John Adams a week and
a half earlier without regret. All that had happened to him as head of

state — and all that had happened before, in his years in the military and as a participant in various political assemblies — all of it at that moment counted as "little more than vanity and vexation." Ahead, he anticipated, lay days in which he could look at life "in the calm lights of mild philosophy."

They would not be as calm as he had hoped. Washington left Mount Vernon for a short time to assume command of American troops when another war with England loomed. No sooner had he assumed his new duties than the prospect faded. He returned home as quickly as he could.

Although he had long been the most famous of Americans, used to the demands of public notice as well as its rewards, Washington now found demands of a different sort in store for him. As Adams cooled the tensions between America and Britain, Washington was not so much settling into his old homestead as he was pulling up to a stage door, about to assume the lead role in a production like none that had ever preceded it in North America. It was a pageant of living history, featuring continuous performances and crowds that did not flag either in attention or number. Washington became a star — however hesitant — of the first magnitude.

On every day of the year when weather permitted, and even when it didn't, men, women, and children made the pilgrimage to Mount Vernon, the new nation's first secular shrine. Most of them idolized Washington — a few were grateful for his long devotion to duty, a few others were perhaps only curious. Some lived nearby, others traveled for several days. The majority were Americans, but there were a few "wide-eyed Europeans" in the crowd from time to time, as well as the occasional South American or Asian. They added up to a huge number.

For the most part, they stood outside a low wall around Mount Vernon, one they could easily have scaled, or they assembled in front of the carriage gate, waiting expectantly. They peered in, eager for a glimpse of Washington as he made his daily rounds, for a nod in passing, perhaps a few words, an acknowledgment of the veneration they had so eagerly come to provide. Most days they saw him. If not, they took satisfaction from simply looking at the home in which Washington lived and, for a few minutes, seeing the same sights that he saw, trying to feel the same serenity that he felt, and imagining the sense of reward that must now be his for having done so much, so well, for his country.

Often they got much more. As odd as it sounds to us today, when celebrities live in fortresses and appear in public surrounded by hordes of bodyguards, Washington didn't merely make himself visible; on occasion he not only talked to his visitors but asked them in for a meal or a tour of the house and grounds. Usually invitations went to those who brought letters of introduction from mutual acquaintances. Sometimes, feeling guilty about admitting some and excluding others, Washington admitted them all — everyone who had assembled on a given day. It was a remarkable display of hospitality on his part, but he thought of it as the least that he could do for people who had gone to so much trouble to pay their respects.

Visitors always accepted the invitation, of course, and were always polite — wiping their shoes before going into the house, speaking quietly, not asking too many questions, not touching what shouldn't be touched. And Washington never complained about anyone breaking something or stealing one of his possessions for a souvenir.

Occasionally after eating he would show his guests one of his medals or a sword or some other object from his military days. He might tell the story behind it, but talking was not what Washington did best, and talking to strangers, especially about himself, was difficult for him. He found it easier to discuss his crops or animals or his plan for a system of canals to link Mount Vernon to the Northwest Territory, thereby encouraging trade among the states and promoting a healthy national economy.

★   ★   ★

But regardless of the subject, people always listened when Washington talked, and in their responses they called him "the General" or "His Excellency." Few referred to him as "the president," and no one ever addressed him as Mr. Washington, much less George.

The amount of time Washington spent with his guests varied, depending on what he had to do that day or how tired he felt. But he always made it known when he had had enough company, and his fans took their cue and promptly departed. It was in some ways, Washington must have thought, like posing for a portrait — so many hours, so much distraction from his own work, all for the purpose of making an impression on strangers. Yet another form of duty.

At times, he longed not to perform it. "Unless some one pops in, unexpectedly," he wrote to his personal secretary in the summer of 1797, "Mrs. Washington and myself will do what I believe has not been [done] within the last twenty years by us, that is to set down to dinner by ourselves."

Unfortunately for Washington, as word of his hospitality spread, more and more people came to seek it and expect it. He was "an indulgent host," writes Gore Vidal. "Unfortunately, neither his wealth nor that of his wife could pay for so royal a way of life. At one point, he seriously considered retreating north to Niagara; if that did not keep his admirers at bay, he was willing to flee even farther into Canada in order to escape his expensive fame. But a few trips away from Mount Vernon made it clear that there was to be no escape for him anywhere; he was to be famous for life and, probably, for all he knew or suspected, thereafter."

Washington had always been a religious man and began, in these last days at home, to think about the hereafter more than he used to. "I was the first, and am now the last of my father's children by the second marriage who remain," he said a few months before he died. "When I shall be called upon to follow them, is known only to the giver of life. When the summons comes I shall endeavor to obey it with good grace."

He had long believed, or claimed to believe, that although he had done his best, history would make up its own mind about him. The matter was out of his hands. "I had rather glide gently down the stream of life," he wrote to his friend and physician James Craik, even before assuming the presidency, "leaving it to posterity to think and say what they please of me, than by any act of mine to have vanity or ostentation imputed to me."

But he is being disingenuous here. He was, after all, a man whose reputation was his most valuable possession, and whose modesty, in addition to being an essential part of his nature, was also a carefully crafted rebuttal to charges of self-absorption. He had heard enough during his lifetime to know what would be said of him after he was gone. "His memory will be adored while liberty shall have votaries," Jefferson wrote in 1784. "His name will triumph over time and will in future ages assume its just station among the most celebrated worthies of the world." Gouverneur Morris, another founder and head of the committee responsible for the final draft of the Constitution, declared: "On his front were enthroned the virtues which exalt, and those which adorn the human character. So dignified his deportment, no man could approach him but with respect — none was great in his presence. . . . In him were the courage of a soldier, the intrepidity of a chief, the fortitude of a hero."

Washington died on December 14, 1799. He was sixty-seven years old. The Senate quickly passed the following resolution in his honor: "The scene is closed — and we are no longer anxious lest misfortune should sully his glory; he has traveled on to the end of his journey, and carried with him an increasing weight of honor: he has deposited it safely where misfortune cannot tarnish it; where malice can not blast it."

The epitaph Washington chose, both for himself and his wife, comes from the Bible, John 11:25–26, "I am the resurrection and the life, saith the Lord, he that believeth in Me, though he were dead, yet shall he live; and whoever liveth and believeth in me shall never die."

He had long since taken the words to heart. Washington believed that his faith entitled him to everlasting life in the realm of the Almighty. And although he would never have admitted it, he surely realized that his achievements on behalf of America entitled him to a different kind of immortality on earth.

Chapter 14
A Message to the Future

*M*ONTICELLO ALSO BECAME A TOURIST ATTRACTION after its owner returned from the presidency, but visitors did not treat it as kindly as Mount Vernon. There were no walls around Jefferson's home and only one fence, meant to protect a vegetable garden from deer. Strangers could tramp right onto the grounds, stroll around, and even sit on Jefferson's verandah as if they belonged there. Sometimes they stood at the windows when Jefferson, his family, and friends were dining. They framed their faces with their hands and mashed their noses against the glass — and occasionally even that was not enough for them. Sometimes they pushed open the front door without knocking and joined those who had congregated inside. The most brazen among them might even chat with Jefferson as if they knew him, as if he had been expecting them. Jefferson, it has been said, "was sometimes not sure whether he was addressing a guest or an interloper."

But some proved worse than interlopers. They vandalized the estate, knocking off corners of brick from the exterior of the house as keepsakes. Others tore at splinters of wood in window frames, doorways, or railings, while still others looked for items lying around that they could slip into their pockets when no one was looking, eager to brag to friends where they had obtained their items. They ignored walkways, tramped over the lawn, and paid no attention to flowers or shrubs.

Such behavior astonished Jefferson. He had never seen anything to compare with it, certainly not in the royal houses of Europe, where tradition regarded heads of state as something close to deities, worshipped from afar, and dispatched to the gallows those who got too crass or too close. Jefferson's pursuit of fame had been dignified, even restrained. He assumed that those who acknowledged his successes would behave similarly. When they did not, it both surprised and saddened him. Eventually, seeing no other choice, he escaped to another residence, almost a hundred miles from Monticello. A few years after his retirement, he began to make the trip twice a year, then three times, then four — seeking the peace he could no longer find at home.

No less annoying to Jefferson was another invasion of his privacy. He had by now resumed his epistolary relationship with John Adams, and one day received a request from a perfect stranger to make the correspondence public. "Would you believe," he wrote to Adams, making no effort to hide his indignation, "that a printer has had the effrontery to propose to me the letting him publish it?"

Adams agreed. "The practice . . . of publishing private Letters without leave, though even as rude ones as mine, is an Abuse and must be reformed." When Adams began to receive notes requesting his own personal writing, he responded, he told Jefferson, either by throwing them away or writing "gruff, short, unintelligible, mysterious, enigmatical, or pedantical Answers" — all variations on "no."

Neither man understood why their confidential musings would interest others or, even if they did, how someone could be so impertinent as to ask for them. If there were thoughts that Jefferson and

Adams wanted to share with their fellow citizens, they would share them, making the decision themselves, not yielding to the pleas of merchants who wanted to disseminate the founders' views not to edify the populace but to fatten their purses. Neither man would have understood the term *celebrity culture*, but in their letters to each other, Jefferson and Adams were among the first Americans to disdain it.

Reflecting on the role he would play in America after his death, Jefferson reminds us of Washington. "I leave others to judge of what I have done," he said, "and to give me exactly that place which they shall think I have occupied. [Chief Justice John] Marshall has written libels on one side; others, I suppose, will be written on the other side; and the world will sift both and separate the truth as well as they can." But his "sincere wish," as he confessed on another occasion, was "that the faithful historian, like the able surgeon, would consider me in his hands, while living, as a dead subject, that the same judgment may now be expressed which will be rendered hereafter, so far as my small agency in human affairs may attract future notice, and I would of choice now stand as at the bar of posterity."

The year before he died, however, he was feeling more confident. He wrote to his friend Joseph C. Cabell, telling him that he expected a kind judgment from history, a long memory, not only for himself but for his fellow founders:

> I have ever found in my progress through life that, acting for the public, if we do always what is right, the approbation denied in the beginning will surely follow us in the end. It is from posterity we are to expect remuneration for the sacrifices we are making for their service, of time, quiet and good will. And I fear not the appeal. The multitude of fine young men whom we shall redeem from ignorance, who will feel that they owe to us the elevation of mind, of character and station they will be able to attain from the result of our efforts, will insure their remembering us with gratitude.

Washington had not feared death because of his religious beliefs. Jefferson did not fear death because, as an avid, lifelong student of science and nature, his library overflowing with volumes on plant and animal life, he had long since made his peace with the inevitability of life's end and the unlikelihood of its continuation in another form. "There is a ripeness of time for death," he wrote to Adams in 1816, a decade before they both died, "regarding others as well as ourselves, when it is reasonable we should drop off, and make room for another growth. When we have lived our generation out, we should not wish to encroach on another."

Jefferson appreciated the unique human ability to realize that life will end and to prepare for it. He might have prepared more than most. Having founded the University of Virginia in his postpresidential years, he left careful plans for its development, explaining in detail how he wanted both the curriculum and the grounds to expand in the decades ahead. In addition, writes biographer Andrew Burstein,

> He took stock of the contents of his wine cellar, gave his "annual gratuity" of twenty dollars each to his favorite slaves . . . and paid his outstanding bills to cover the requirements of daily existence, such as newspapers and bookbinding and repair of his prized "polygraph," the mechanical device that enabled him to produce instantaneous copies of outgoing letters. He made sure that his private papers were perfectly filed and readily accessible to his thirty-three-year-old grandson and executor, Thomas Jefferson Randolph. He knew how he wanted to embark on his voyage into historical memory.

And he knew precisely what he wanted that memory to be. His epitaph could have listed any number of achievements, enough to have required a much larger stone. Instead, he limited himself to three:

Here was buried
Thomas Jefferson
Author of the Declaration of American Independence,
Of the Statute of Virginia for Religious Freedom,
And Father of the University of Virginia.

He might not be able to control what people said of him after he was gone, but he could certainly make his wishes known. He could inform them that he did not want to be remembered for the political decisions he had made as governor of Virginia, many of which had been roundly criticized, or as president of the United States, many of which had been highly praised. Nor did he want history to think of him as John Adams's vice president. Rather, he hoped to live on for what he had accomplished intellectually, what he had conceived in his mind and set down on parchment and in the blueprints that became university buildings, themselves dedicated to intellectual accomplishment.

These were the most significant claims to fame of a man who could never really decide whether it was proper to make such claims.

Chapter 15
John Adams Survives

J EFFERSON AND ADAMS BOTH DIED JULY 4, 1826, the fiftieth anniversary of the signing of the Declaration of Independence. It is the most famous coincidence in the history of the republic. Jefferson died early in the afternoon. A few hours later, Adams is supposed to have muttered weakly, and incorrectly, "Thomas Jefferson survives." Not long after that, he, too, passed away. The two men had been writing to each other about the end of their lives for more than a decade.

Jefferson: "Our machines have now been running for 70. or 80. years, and we must expect that, worn as they are, here a pivot, there a wheel, now a pinion, next a spring, will be giving way and however we may tinker them up for awhile, all will at length surcease motion."

Adams: "I am sometimes afraid that my 'machine' will not 'surcease motion' soon enough; for I dread nothing so much as 'dying at top' and expiring like Dean Swift 'a driveller and a Show' or like

Sam. Adams, a Grief and distress to his Family, a weeping helpless Object of Compassion for Years."

To some, however, it was no coincidence that Adams and Jefferson died within hours of each other. It had to be something more, a sign of "Divine favor," as John Quincy Adams wrote in his diary that night — the Almighty's way of recognizing all that the two founders, friends turned enemies turned friends, had accomplished in their lives. It was a kind of blessing on the country they had done so much to bring into being.

To Americans who knew of it, their virtually simultaneous deaths were a source of wonder. William Wirt, John Quincy's attorney general and Patrick Henry's biographer, was among the many to offer a joint eulogy: "In the structure of their characters; in the course of their action; in the striking coincidences which marked their high career; in the lives and deaths of the illustrious men, whose virtues and services we have met to commemorate — and in that voice of admiration and gratitude which has since burst, with one accord, from the twelve millions of freemen who people these States, there is a moral sublimity which overwhelms the mind, and hushes all its powers into silent amazement!"

And Daniel Webster, the statesman and Patrick Henry's equal as an orator, lamented that "Adams and Jefferson are no more. On our fiftieth anniversary, the great day of the National Jubilee, in the very hour of public rejoicing, in the midst of echoing and re-echoing voices of thanksgiving, while their own names were on all tongues, they took their flight, together, to the world of spirits."

Unlike Jefferson, Adams didn't write an epitaph. We don't know why, although we can certainly rule out modesty as well as an unshakable confidence that posterity would keep him in mind without prompting. It may be that, like so many, as he aged, Adams questioned the priorities of his earlier years. It may be that, in looking back, he couldn't make sense of the ambitious young man he had been — all those hours poring over law books, the prospect of renown a beacon shining for him in the distance. It may be that, as

1826 approached, the pursuit of fame seemed to him no longer worth the price he had had to pay, nor the harboring of jealousy or expression of vanity. Adams had expended more energy on the ingredients of renown than any other founder. When the time came to assess all that striving, to summarize it for a slab of granite, he might have been too weary to bother. Or so certain of having done all he could that there was no point in further reflection.

Also more than the other founders, Adams had family matters on his mind as the end drew near — more than enough to distract him from himself. His beloved wife Abigail had died in 1818, and it was the greatest shock of his life. "Gracious God!" wrote John Quincy on hearing the news. "Support my father in this deep and irreparable affliction." It is not clear that God ever did, or could have. Adams was inconsolable. "I wish I could lay beside her and die, too," he said in her last hours, and when those hours were over he seemed for a time to have departed with her.

The loss of his son Charles, who had drunk himself to death some years earlier at the age of thirty, also troubled him. Adams was angry at the extent to which his son had abused himself, angry at Charles's refusal to listen to repeated pleas from his father to give up the bottle. But had Adams done all he could? Surely some of the blame for the child's dissipation lies with the parent, no matter how much effort the parent has made. Adams wondered what he had done wrong, what he might have done differently, whether his son's fate augured darkly for his other descendants. Would ignominy, not fame, be the patrimony of John Adams's line?

His much more accomplished son, John Quincy, was elected president in 1824. The father thought the son had performed capably in office but sensed that the electorate disagreed. The problem, Adams believed, was not just that war hero Andrew Jackson was waiting in the wings, stirring up the people to vote for him in the next election, nor was it John Quincy's competence, which was all that the job required and more. The problem, Adams thought, was his manner. John Quincy did not impress with his appearance or inspire with his words. Adams had passed his lack of style along to his son. He feared that John Quincy would be dismissed from office after a single term just as he had been, and he was right. A man naturally thinks of his legacy in the last years of his life. It may be that Adams was too discouraged for prolonged musing.

So Joseph J. Ellis did some musing for him. Writing in 1993, he wondered what Adams would have made of what history had made of him. What if he had been able to rise from the grave and drop into late-twentieth-century America? Ellis imagines that Adams

> would probably derive a perverse sense of satisfaction in correctly predicting his own relative obscurity, noting for the record that no major mausoleums, monuments, or statues had yet been erected in his honor. In a final spasm of candor and irreverence, he might ask if his beloved republic, now in its third century of existence, had reached a sufficiently ripened stage of development to acknowledge his present relevance. Explaining in his defensive and over-animated way that he did not want to be famous so much as useful, he might propose the construction of an Adams monument on the Tidal Basin in the nation's capital, done in the classical style and situated sufficiently close to the Jefferson Memorial that, depending on the time of day and angle of the sun, he and Jefferson might take turns casting shadows across each other's facades.

But there is no such monument. There is only the family crypt at the United First Parish Church in Quincy, Massachusetts. Adams's name appears outside the crypt on a plaque put up in 1900 by members of the John Adams Chapter of the Daughters of the American Revolution, and they wrote the inscription. Like Jefferson's, it summed up a lifetime in three encompassing categories:

JOHN ADAMS
SIGNER OF THE DECLARATION OF INDEPENDENCE
FRAMER OF THE CONSTITUTION OF MASSACHUSETTS
SECOND PRESIDENT OF THE UNITED STATES
1735—1826

Shortly after the unveiling ceremony, one of the members of the DAR chapter said she thought Adams would have approved, both of the accomplishments chosen and the simplicity of the wording. He was not a showy man, this John Adams. He would not have wanted anything ostentatious, either in sentiment or in size.

Actually, as a much younger man, Adams had written an epitaph — but not for himself. It was carved into the sarcophagus lid of the first member of his family to arrive in Massachusetts, Henry Adams, who landed in what is now Massachusetts in 1638. Said John about his ancestor:

> This stone and several others have been placed in this yard by a great, great grandson from a veneration of the piety, humility, simplicity, prudence, frugality, industry and perseverance of his ancestors in hopes of recommending an affirmation of their virtues to their posterity.

As it turned out, despite misgivings that tormented him for much of his life, it was John Adams, not his ancestor, whose virtues were most recommended to posterity.

Epilogue
The Autograph of a Not-So-Famous Man

*D*ESPITE INITIAL IMPRESSIONS, and the examples in the previous pages, there are similarities between the nature of celebrity in the eighteenth and twenty-first centuries. In both, those who held important positions in government were famous, and in both, fame meant extra income after they departed from public service and capitalized on their names. End of comparisons. Total: two — and they cannot be expressed without caveats.

In the eighteenth century, fame graced public officials for their accomplishments and eluded them for incompetence or venality, which is to say that, in most cases, it had more to do with the quality of the man than with the status of the position, and the man was judged according to the strictest of standards.

In the twenty-first century, all politicians are celebrities of one sort or another. Because media outlets have insatiable appetites and standards are so lax as not to be standards at all, today's politicians control their visibility: they call press conferences, appear on TV talk shows, take calls from listeners on radio talk shows, give sound bites on the run, confide in newspaper and magazine reporters eager to fill column inches, update their Web sites more often than necessary, send mailings to constituents boasting of their deeds, record their voices for automated phone calls, make public appearances and then arrange for the appearances to be covered on TV, radio, the Internet, and in print — one form of publicity feeding another, the whole public persona growing larger than the sum of its parts.

The media, in all their numerous forms, make politicians famous today, regardless of ability, commitment, or integrity. Exposure, not merit, controls renown — the same in government as in show business.

As for the money that political figures can make once they return to private life, the similarity between eras is minimal. For a short time after the Parson's Cause, and then again after his various duties associated with the Revolutionary War and his terms as governor of Virginia, Patrick Henry prospered by taking on more clients than he had before and raising his fees. The same held true for Alexander Hamilton after his tenure as secretary of the treasury. But neither man became wealthy. Henry depended on the income from his crops at Red Hill, and Hamilton eventually combined his law practice with ownership and editorial control of the *New-York Evening Post.*

These days, a retired cabinet officer or congressman can make a fortune without even having a job. All he has to do is give the same speech time and again to groups that pay exorbitant fees so that they can publish his name on their programs and allow their members to pose for pictures with him as they sip cocktails afterward, the bonhomie so false that the photos seem a form of caricature. It doesn't matter what the celebrity says, only that he appears on the dais and poses afterward with the faithful — and that the group that hosts him buys a few thousand copies of his memoir as party favors so that the book jumps for one week onto the *New York Times* best-seller list.

But there are greater differences between the two periods than these, and they are even more troubling. With a few notable exceptions, the most famous people in the world today don't address the world's most pressing needs. Rather, they distract us from them. They provide amusement, not sustenance. They do not make us think. They wave brightly colored pieces of fabric in front of our eyes and hope that we will delight ourselves in the swirls of motion as if we were children — easily fascinated, hungry for diversion. Heads of charitable institutions are not famous, but performers with electronically augmented voices are. Scientists seeking cures for diseases are not famous, but vulgar comedians are. Educators trying to improve the lot of their students are not famous, but actors who play supporting roles in computer-generated movies are. Philosophers are not famous, but shooting guards who can get their own shots off the dribble are. It is a familiar plaint.

But at least these athletes and entertainers have a skill and give pleasure to those who watch them, even if the pleasure is fleeting and far too much is made of it. There is also today a subspecies of celebrities who do not give pleasure in any conventional sense, whose fame is based not on ability but on itself. A person can become famous because of behavior that is pointless, loutish, or even criminal, or because he happened to be the victim of such behavior. The words *famous* and *notorious*, which have opposite meanings, are becoming synonymous, and it can only be regarded as the most telling of ironies: the ignorance of those who use the words incorrectly has come to reflect a social reality that proper usage altogether misses. If fame is still a club, as it might have been to Patrick Henry, membership requirements have sunk so low that you only have to twist the doorknob to get in.

In retrospect, it all seems predictable. The crowds that gathered at Mount Vernon provided the first clue that celebrities would eventually become too important to their fans, that the fans would seek some kind of inappropriate proximity as a result. The people who besieged Monticello provided the first clue that the fans would sometimes behave raucously in the presence of their idols, the sheer energy of their admiration overwhelming their better judgment. And the demand for paintings of Alexander Hamilton after his death provided the first clue that the veneration of the individual would transmogrify into a craving for commercial artifacts.

But before any of this there was another clue. You can find it in the story of the most improbably named founder of them all, and one of the few to end up even less famous than poor James Wilson.

It took Button Gwinnett a while to believe that the colonies could, or should, free themselves from British rule. After all, he had been born in the motherland, had been educated there, had met and married his wife there, and once he came to America in the early 1760s and settled in South Carolina, he made his living trading with England, becoming so successful that he was able to purchase a large parcel of St. Catherine's Island, off the coast of Georgia, and build a profitable plantation there. He corresponded with friends across the ocean and kept up with the news from London and other cities in the empire.

But by 1775 he had come to believe that the Crown's policies, especially with regard to taxation, were so misguided as to be fomenting rebellion, and that only by opposing them could the colonies — and businessmen like himself — survive. At the outset, Gwinnett merely complained to his fellow businessmen. Then he began to work at a solution. First, he was elected to the Georgia General Assembly, and after that to Congress, drawing up legislation to restrict British control of America. Later, Gwinnett became one of the principal authors of Georgia's constitution. He would never have imagined himself taking so active a role against the nation of his birth, but circumstances, he believed, had forced his hand. He didn't like it, but he was committed. The British had to allow colonists more freedom to rule themselves.

"In his person," writes nineteenth-century historian Charles A. Goodrich, "Mr. Gwinnett was tall, and of noble and commanding appearance." When he spoke, "his language . . . was mild, and . . . his

manners polite and graceful," but "in his temper, he was irritable" —
and that, it turned out, was his undoing.

Once the Revolutionary War started, British troops destroyed
Gwinnett's property. Seeking revenge, he asked to be named
brigadier general of the Georgia militia, a position for which he was
well qualified. Also well qualified was a gentleman named Lackland
M'Intosh, and he, too, wanted to head the colony's troops. After
much debate in the assembly, the appointment went to M'Intosh, a
decision, says Goodrich, that "Mr. Gwinnett bore with little fortitude. His ambition was disappointed, and being naturally hasty in his
temper, and in his conclusions, he seems, from this time, to have
regarded Colonel M'Intosh as a personal enemy."

Shortly afterward, perhaps in an attempt to make amends to
Gwinnett, Georgia officials elected him president of the colony's
most powerful body, the Executive Council. He accepted the post
gratefully, swore he would execute its duties to the best of his abilities, and then started in on what he obviously regarded as the most
important duty of all: making life as difficult as possible for M'Intosh
and the men he commanded.

On one occasion, Gwinnett forbade M'Intosh to lead the militia on an expedition against the British in the eastern part of Florida. M'Intosh was not up to the task, Gwinnett declared, and then
announced that he, Gwinnett, would assume the command himself.
He thought that as head of the Executive Council he was entitled to
take such a step. In fact, the opposite was true. He was specifically
forbidden, ex officio, to march into battle. M'Intosh resumed his
preparations for battle.

Undaunted, Gwinnett came up with plan B. Instead of returning the command to M'Intosh for the Florida expedition, he pro-
moted one of the colonel's subordinates to head the mission.
M'Intosh had no choice but to accept the demotion, but he was
furious — all the more so when the mission failed because of the
faulty leadership. The blame went to Gwinnett. M'Intosh and scores

of others accused him of sabotaging his own colony's best interests for no other reason than vengeance. It was the end of his political career, a judgment confirmed shortly afterward when he ran for governor and soundly lost. M'Intosh shed no tears. But, Goodrich writes: "In the disappointment and mortification of his adversary, General M'Intosh foolishly exulted."

Gwinnett responded with equal foolishness, following an all too familiar ritual of the era: they exchanged insults, issued threats, the threats escalated, and finally, inevitably, Gwinnett challenged M'Intosh to a duel.

On March 27, 1777, less than a year after Gwinnett had earned a place in history by signing the Declaration of Independence, he and his adversary faced each other at a distance of only twelve feet. They chose their pistols, examined them, and aimed. The count began. Gwinnett glared at M'Intosh, and M'Intosh glared at Gwinnett. Seconds later they fired. M'Intosh was seriously wounded. Gwinnett, forty-five years old, was killed.

Georgians paid their respects to the deceased — but not for long. There was, after all, a war going on, and, besides, Gwinnett was not well known in some circles and not well respected in others. To this day, many Georgians have never heard of Button Gwinnett, and no one knows for certain where he is buried. His grave marker in Colonial Cemetery in Savannah informs that his remains "are believed to lie entombed hereunder."

The period of grieving over, a few of the colonists got down to business. They collected all the signatures of Gwinnett they could get their hands on — some affixed to legal and governmental documents, some on personal correspondence — and sold them for as much as the market would bear. There had been no value to Button Gwinnett's autograph before he died, his signature attracting no more posthumous attention than the signature of any other Georgian public official.

Then everything changed. People not only began to pay for Gwinnett's autograph, but, as time passed, they paid more and more.

The man might have been dead, but his value was alive and growing. Today, if a Button Gwinnett signature surfaced, it would go for as much as a Henry Clay, a John Calhoun, and a James Polk put together.

It didn't matter that Gwinnett wasn't a noteworthy figure, that he didn't invent instruments or institutions, didn't lead large and imposing organizations, didn't write great words, or, as far as anybody knows, think great thoughts. What mattered was that bizarre circumstance had intruded into his life, ending it ignobly and thereby separating him from the ranks of the ordinary. He was the first signer of the Declaration of Independence to have died violently, and that made him — even in an age that should have known better — a figure of renown.

Button Gwinnett was the first pointless celebrity in American history. There would be many more, for even less sensible reasons, in the centuries to come.

ACKNOWLEDGMENTS

Debbie Celia, of the Westport Public Library in Connecticut, was indispensable to my previous volume on colonial America, *Infamous Scribblers*. She was even more so to this book, since much of the source material was online and my skills do not lie in that direction. Hers do, and I am exceedingly grateful.

To the best of my knowledge, *Virtue, Valor, & Vanity* is the first book written specifically about the attitude of the founders toward fame, which made the research all the more demanding and precise. I am, for that reason, also exceedingly grateful to the following: Anna Berkes, research librarian, Thomas Jefferson Library, Monticello; Toni Carter, assistant librarian, Virginia Historical Society; Beth Chute, manager of promotion and public relations, Trinity Church-St. Paul's Chapel, New York; Karen Gorham-Smith, associate curator, Patrick Henry National Memorial; Marie Hogan, John Adams Papers, Massachusetts Historical Society; Mandi Johnson, Georgia Historical Society; Jennifer Kittlaus, library assistant, Mount Vernon; Jon Kukla, curator, Patrick Henry National Memorial; Greg Lint, editor, John

Adams Papers, Massachusetts Historical Society; Kate Ohno, assistant editor, Benjamin Franklin Papers, Yale University; Frances Pollard, Virginia Historical Society; Greg Stoner, reference department manager, Virginia Historical Society.

I also heartily thank Dick Seaver and his associates at Arcade Publishing, most notably James Jayo. And no less heartily, my eloquent and caring agent, Tim Seldes.

NOTES

When quoting from the collected works of one of the founders, I am almost always excerpting a letter, and in the note I give the date of the letter, which is most likely what the reader wants to know. But there are exceptions. In those few cases where I am not excerpting a letter from someone's collected works, but different material, such as a reminiscence from John Adams's autobiography, which shares a four-volume set with his diary, or a passage from the three-volume *Life, Correspondence, and Speeches of Patrick Henry*, I do not give the date. Sometimes the date is not apparent: who knows, for instance, when Adams wrote specific passages of his autobiography? Sometimes it is not certain: the occasions for some of Henry's speeches are guesswork more than fact. In these cases, I have provided volume and page number. This method, I believe, is the easiest way for readers to find the passages in question, whatever their specific source.

Introduction: *The Crew of the* Concord

ix   *many pleasant Islands . . . affords also Materials for Dying*   Harris, p. 816.

Chapter 1: The Roman Republic

3   *a stability missing*   Lind, p. 47.

3   *the Roman constitution*   Ibid., pp. 47–48.

4   *the very name*   Lind, p. 48.

5   *Come here, soldier*   Everitt, p. 318.

6   *masterpieces of popularization*   Ibid., p. 322.

6   *When Marcus was about to launch*   Ibid., p. 24.

6   *fame and good men's praises*   Braudy, p. 79.

7   *Despite the fact*   Everitt, p. 33.

7   *Once I had realized*   Ibid., p. 70.

7   *with full lips*   Ibid., p. 3.

8   *Public esteem is the nurse*   Braudy, p. 55.

8   *intemperately fond*   Ibid., p. 73.

8   *By his insatiable thirst*   Ibid., p. 73.

9   *I brought the house down*   Everitt, p. 126.

9   *The striving for praise*   Braudy, p. 77.

9   *In all history*   McCullough, *Adams*, p. 375.

10   *in future ages*   PJA, February 13, 1760.

10   *Such a man*   Richard, p. 61.

11   *There was never any great man*   PBF, 3:337.

11   *among the most valuable treatises*   Ibid., p. 36.

Chapter 2: The American in Paris

13   *He could not drink*   Morgan, p. 6.

14   *He stole the fire*   Wood, p. 172.

15   *For a man of seventy*   Brands, pp. 523–24.

16   *there was scarcely*   McCullough, *Adams*, p. 193.

16   *paraded no utopias*   Durant, p. 869.

17   *The celebrated Franklin* and *Doctor Franklin*   Brands, p. 528.

17   *Reputedly, the King himself*   McCullough, *Adams*, pp. 193–94.

18   *Is that white hat*   Isaacson, p. 348.

18   *à la Franklin*   Durant, p. 905.

19   *Every day I shall remember*   Isaacson, p. 433.

19   *We were received*   Ibid., p. 437.

20   *The affectionate welcome*   Ibid., p. 438.

20   *These, with the pictures*   Braudy, p. 454.

21   *And with what rare Inventions*   PBF, 4:88.

21   *imitate Jesus and Socrates*   Adair, p. 7.

21   *The hope of acquiring*   PBF, 3:437.

22   *Long had we*   Ibid., 10:424.

23   *Love of Praise and it reigns more or less*   Ibid., September 12, 1751.

23   *egotism transmuted gloriously*   Adair, p. 12.

Chapter 3: Americans at Home

25   *the period is more distant*   Ellis, *Brothers*, p. 94.

26   *The love of honest*   Wills, *Cincinnatus*, p. 129.

26   *The wisest and most benign*   WJW, p. 238.

26   *The love of reputation*   Wills, *Cincinnatus*, p. 129.

26   *I will not appeal to vanity*   WJW, p. 237.

27   *What . . . can be intrinsically*   Richard, p. 65.

28   *managed to squeeze from stones*   McCloskey, introduction to *WJW*, p. 44.

28   *hunted like a wild beast*   Ibid., p. 44.

29   *In offering my respects*   WGW, July 4, 1780.

29   *To be sure*   Ellis, *Excellency*, p. 77.

30   *Thee, first in peace*   Untermeyer, pp. 130–31.

30   *an almost uninterrupted series*   Brookhiser, *Father*, p 73.

30   *Virgins fair*   Ibid., p. 73.

30   *Far be the din of arms*   *Gazette of the United States*, April 25, 1789.

31   *constantly testing public opinion*   Wills, *Cincinnatus*, p. 103.

31   *Whensoever I shall be convinced*   Woods, p. 46.

31   *the Malice of your worst Enemies*   PGW, July 14, 1776.

32   *inexpressible concern*   PGW, June 18, 1775.

32   *to hear from different Quarters*   Schwartz, p. 89.

33   *Washington said*   Flexner, *Revolution*, p. 524.

33   *Be easy*   PGW, November 10, 1775.

34   *is polite with dignity*   Hannaford, p. 4.

34   *No person*   Flexner, *New Nation*, p. 6.

34   *the greatest man in the world*   Ferling, p. 255.

35   *Seeking fame*   Well, p. 428.

35   *the Man who nobly vindicates*   Alexander, p. 95.

36   *a golden-haired*   Ellis, *Sphinx*, p. 93.

37   *Head . . . You confess your follies*   TJL, October 12, 1786.

37   *Head . . . see what you suffer*   Ibid.

38   *Head . . . To avoid those eternal distresses*   Ibid.

39   *that government is best*   Brodie, p. 25.

39   *The less we say*   Bailyn, p. 499.

39   *one of the most unpopular*   David, p. 108.

39   *a pusillanimous and morbid terror*   Mayo, p. 50.

39   *of mixed aspect*   Malone, *Sage*, p. 225.

40   *to pursue the interests* and *fame and promotion*   TJL, August 19, 1785.

40   *present fame*   Ibid., January 11, 1816.

40   *which would have been deemed honorable*   Ibid., February 10, 1810.

40   *His foible*   Ibid., January 30, 1787.

40   *and a reputation*   TJL, December 28, 1822.

41   *They replied*   DAJA, 3:270.

41   *exercises my lungs*   McCullough, p. 45.

41   *It will be hard work*   PJA, August 29, 1756.

42   *In exchange for the hours*   Grant, p. 34.

42   *Reputation ought to be*   DAJA, March 14, 1759.

43   *In short*   Ibid., June 10, 1760.

43   *Asylum of all the discontented*   AFP, November 26, 1794.

43   *No man is entirely free*   Kagle, p. 162.

43   *is miserable every moment*   Woods, p. 182.

44   *Noisy applause*   PJA, February 1760. Adams did not date this letter more specifically. It seems to have been written on the thirteenth or a few days afterward.

44   *I have received such Blessings*   DAJA, June 28, 1770.

44   *I cannot say*   AFP, January 24, 1793.

45   *Above the mists*   Ibid., January 10, 1795.

45   *Deeply touched*   Ibid., pp. 500–501.

46   *Our attachment to Character*   Ibid., January 7, 1793.

47   *will add the inducements*   FP, 1:87.

48   *the ruling passion*   Ibid., 72:414.

48   *never appeared solicitous*   Woods, p. 230.

48   *so exuberant was the lionization*   Chernow, p. 269.

49   *We have you exhibited here*   PAH, August 15, 1791.

49   *the most remarkable generation*   Schlesinger, p. 245.

49   *hero worship is the cult*   Hughes-Hallett, p. 7.

50   *Heroes expose themselves*   Ibid., p. 13.

50   *one of the wild ones and readiness to risk*   Ibid., p. 22.

50   *turning his back*   Hughes-Hallett, p. 147–48.

51   *Historical heroes*   Ibid., p. 7.

52   *a man with*   Ibid., pp. 55–56.

52   *a hero must be able*   Ibid., p. 10.

52   *overall avidity and brightness*   Randall, p. 45.

Chapter 4: Ambition

57   *civic narcissism*   Braudy, p. 368.

58   *that laudable Ambition*   GWP, September 1, 1758.

58   *It would be a happy pride*   Ibid., July 4, 1777.

58   *it will ever be*   Ibid., April 18, 1776.

58   *I have always believed*   JMP, August 25, 1826.

58 *combination of bottomless ambition* Ellis, *Excellency*, p. 38.

59 *With the vanishing* Flexner, *Nation*, pp. 8–9.

60 *To merit the Approbation* GWP, February 10, 1783

60 *The little spice* JMP, April 27, 1795.

60 *I have no ambition* Ibid., December 28, 1796.

61 *to confess my weakness* WAH, November 11, 1769.

62 *After the cloth* Adair, p. 13.

62 *vaulting ambition* Chernow, p. 554.

62 *an ambition to excel* PAH, July 28, 1784.

62 *That he is ambitious* Chernow, p. 559.

63 *Sometime last fall* and *to avoid the embarrassment* PAH, November 22, 1780.

63 *The desire for reward* Adair, p. 8.

63 *The first way* McCullough, *Adams*, p. 46.

64 *he imagined* Grant, p. 4.

66 *He told me* DAJA, 3:282–83.

66 *Of that Ambition* AFP, March 16, 1777.

66 *Let us have Ambition* Ibid., June 17, 1777.

66 *Is it possible* BFP, November 27, 1761.

67 *insatiable ambition* *Columbian Centinel*, September 20, 1800.

67 *These are my pretensions* PAH, May 2, 1781.

67 *perverted ambition* FP, 1:88.

67 *assaults of ambition* Ibid., 70:402.

67 *the ambition or enmity* Ibid., 34: 228.

67 *ambitious, vindictive, and rapacious* Ibid., 5:104.

67 *ambition and jealousy* Ibid., 8:117.

67 *ambition or revenge* Ibid., 30:216.

67 *sacred knot which binds* Ibid., 15:145.

68 *at last takes possession* Woods, p. 182.

68 *the horrid Figures* AFP, April 16, 1783.

68 *lawless ambition* GWP, March 1, 1778.

68	*the mercenary instruments* Ibid., January 30, 1781.
68	*the folly and madness* Ibid., December 13, 1783.
68	*ambition & intrigues* JMP, January 15, 1797.
68	*ambition & self-Interest* Ibid., August 23, 1785.
68	*ambition or corruption* Ibid., November 27, 1830.
68	*greedy ambition* Ibid., July 29, 1803.
68	*this happy people* and *precipitated by the rage* LCSPH, June 7, 1788.
70	*Superb sermons* Brooks, pp. 93–94.
71	*not worth a copper* Mayo, p. 10.
73	*from being the father* Ibid., p. 19.
73	*We have heard* LCSPH, 1:41.
74	*The gentleman has spoken treason* Morgan, p. 71.
74	*taken captive* Beeman, p. 19
74	*was emphatic without vehemence* Ibid., p. 25.
74	*was the perfect master* Ibid., p. 25.
74	*Some twenty minutes* Morgan, p. 70.
75	*little petty-fogging attorney* Beeman, p. 20.
76	*After the court* Wirt, 1:43–44.

Chapter 5: Vanity

79	*flatters my vanity* Isaacson, p. 461.
80	*Having emerg'd from the Poverty* Franklin, p. 3.
80	*And last* Ibid., p. 4.
81	*Washington has something* Brookhiser, *Father*, pp. 108–9.
82	*Mr. Parish is at work* Murray, p. 123.
82	*the neatest and best* Ibid.
82	*in want of as much* Ibid.
82	*as much superfine* Ibid., p. 124.
83	*stately journeying* Tebbel and Watts, p. 16.
83	*highly flattering to my vanity* GWP, April 28, 1782.

83   *I thank you most sincerely*   Ibid., February 28, 1776.

84   *the bosom of my family* and *my farm, my books*   TJL, April 25, 1794.

84   *I shall escape*   Ibid., January 30, 1797.

84   *Politics, as well as religion*   Meacham, pp. 73–74.

85   *examined well my heart*   TJL, May 20, 1782.

86   *indiscreet, vain and opinionated*   Brookhiser, *Hamilton*, p. 7.

86   *egotism and vanity*   Chernow, p. 624.

86   *weakness, vanity*   Ibid., p. 625.

86   *littleness of mind*   DAJA, 1:73.

87   *insolent coxcomb*   Ibid., p. 334.

87   *had been blown up with vanity*   Ibid., p. 521–22.

87   *I have found him sober*   PAH, October 29, 1790.

87   *One evening*   Brookhiser, *Hamilton*, p. 185.

88   *a ridiculous display*   McCullough, *Adams*, p. 269.

88   *I know the unflinching character*   Ibid., pp. 268–69.

88   *The charge of vanity* and *I have long since learned*   Ibid., p. 269.

89   *hates Franklin*   Ibid., p. 318.

89   *I'll tell in a trice*   Ibid., p. 408.

89   *Whenever Vanity, and Gaiety*   AFP, April 14, 1776.

90   *As the Lives of Phylosophers*   Ibid., October 5, 1802.

90   *My Life has been too trifling*   AJL, May 29, 1813.

90   *Vanity, I am sensible*   PJA, April 16, 1801.

Chapter 6: Modesty

91   *came home in great Anxiety*   DAJA, February 15, 1771.

92   *had exhausted my health*   Ibid., 3:296.

92   *What an Atom*   Grant, p. 100.

92   *a great Truth*   DAJA, 4:14.

93   *A Man must be selfish*   AFP, August 18, 1776.

93   *No man better merited*   McCullough, *Adams*, p. 135.

93   *Men of extraordinary Fame*   DAJA, 3:253.

93   *Let the Butterflies of Fame*   AFP, July 8, 1777.

93   *I know the voice of Fame*   Ibid., December 9, 1781.

94   *lived a cheerful country life . . . I am not insensible*   New England Courant, April 2, 1722.

95   *faithful assistant* and *modesty and love of concord*   Chernow, p. 92.

96   *Is it you, sir*   JC, Washington ed., iii, p. 213.

96   *Political power*   Ellis, *Sphinx*, p. 192–93.

97   *Caesar had his Brutus*   John Bartlett, *Familiar Quotations*, 14th ed. (Boston: Little, Brown, 1968), p. 464.

97   *The gentlemen may cry*   Ibid., p. 465.

98   *first in war*   Ibid., p. 486.

100   *Mr. President*   PGW, June 16, 1755.

100   *I am now Imbarked*   Ibid., June 19, 1775.

101   *I have often thought*   Ibid., January 14, 1776.

102   *Let me conjure you then*   Ibid., May 22, 1782.

103   *under the shadow*   WP, February 1, 1788.

103   *the increasing infirmities*   Ibid., April 28, 1788.

103   *the extravagant*   Tebbel, p. 57.

104   *Gentlemen, the gratification*   PGW, May 3, 1791.

104   *expressions of satisfaction*   Ibid., May 30, 1791.

Chapter 7: Jealousy

107   *If ever any Man*   PBF, July 29, 1778.

108   *was a somewhat farcical night*   Isaacson, p. 318–19.

108   *may possibly be spread* and *when shut up together*   Ibid., p. 264.

108   *harrangue* and *I was so much*   DAJA, 3:418.

108   *The next Morning*   Ibid., 3:419.

109   *the famous Adams*   Ellis, *Sage*, p. 11.

109   *A man must be*   Vidal, p. 61.

110   *Dr. Franklin was reported*   AFP, April 16, 1778.

110   *I neither then nor ever since*   Ibid., April 19, 1778.

110 *That [Franklin] was a great Genius* Ibid., April 21, 1778.

111 *the best part of two Years* Ibid., April 9, 1778.

111 *a Passion for Reputation* DAJA, 2:367.

111 *a great philosopher* Brands, p. 548.

112 *I can now inform you* DAJA, June 17, 1775.

112 *Washington is in the right* Ibid., April 13, 1777.

114 *Mr. Jefferson* Ibid., 3:335.

115 *I have so long been* Ibid., December 26, 1793.

115 *a good riddance* Ibid., January 6, 1794.

117 *Hamilton has made* Ibid., December 13, 1795.

117 *Hamilton I know* AFP, January 9, 1797.

118 *the most restless* Brookhiser, *Hamilton*, pp. 139–40.

119 *account with John Hancock* Grant, p. 107.

119 *saw in Mr. Hancock* DAJA, 3:305.

120 *I regarded it very little* Ibid., 3:305.

120 *indulged their jealousies so far* Ibid., 3:324.

121 *Mr. Hancock* Ibid., 3:324.

121 *Jealousy is as cruel as the Grave* AFP, May 14, 1782.

122 *You say that Washington* SF, August 23, 1805.

122 *All of this* Ibid., September 30, 1805.

122 *Oratory in this age?* Ibid., July 23, 1806.

123 *When my parson says* Ibid., February 25, 1808.

123 *I shall turn* and *The Declaration of Independence* and *I think I may boast* Ibid., June 21, 1811.

123 *I ought to have mentioned* Ibid., July 8, 1812.

124 *I am weary* Ibid., March 23, 1809.

125 *useful inferences* McCullough, *Adams*, p. 600.

126 *A letter from you* Ibid., p. 603.

126 *You may expect* AJL, June 10, 1813.

126 *I have thus stated* Ibid., October 28, 1813.

127 *Franklin had a great genius* Isaacson, p. 477–78.

Chapter 8: Image

129   *Speaking generally*   MCullough, *Adams*, p. 638.

129   *ingenious* and *has Vanity*   Garrett, p. 248.

130   *lets me do*   Oliver, p. 189.

130   *The age of sculpture*   Ibid., p. 1.

130   *Sir, There are several things*   Ibid., pp. 145–46.

130   *candor, probity, and decision*   McCullough, *Adams*, p. 344.

130   *no small amount of vanity*   Meschutt, p. 77.

131   *I have taken the liberty*   Fisher, p. 389.

131   *Instead of lying flat on the back*   Millard, p. 71.

132   *He did not tear my face*   Ibid., p. 642.

132   *Every student and reader*   Oliver, p. 1.

133   *In the process*   Malone, *Sage*, pp. 469–70.

133   *perfect facsimile* and *a faithful and living Likeness*   Goodwin and Bear, p. 7.

133   *vile plasterer*   Malone, *Sage*, p. 469.

133   *wax, plaster, and marble*   Goodwin and Bear, p. 5.

134   *I am duly sensible*   JC, Washington ed., 7:203.

134   *had been on terms of confidence*   Trumbull, p. 173.

134   *a very fine thing* and *deemed the best*   Goodwin and Bear, p. 6.

134   *Of the merit of these*   Barratt and Miles, p. 281.

135   *I am not qualified*   Goodwin and Bear, p. 5.

135   *a few broad strokes*   Peterson, p. 8.

135   *There was no 'standard likeness'*   Peterson, p. 245.

135   *no feature*   Goodwin and Bear, p. 7.

136   *Mr. Adams will write you*   AJL, July 10, 1787.

137   *desirous of expressing*   PAH, December 29, 1791.

137   *appear unconnected*   Cooper, p. 122.

138   *a brisk energy*   Chernow, p. 2.

138   *a financial godsend*   Trumbull, p. 237n4.

138   *The feelings of the whole community*   Chernow, p. 710.

138   *there was as much*   Ibid., p. 710.

139   *was kept in comfortable employment*   Trumbull, p. 237n4.

139   *was not in appearance*   Van Doren, p. 260.

139   *He is of the first Reputation*   PBF, October 26, 1785.

139   *the pleasure I shall receive*   Ibid., May 24, 1780.

140   *I have at the request*   Ibid., June 25, 1780.

140   *a testimony*   Ibid., December 31, 1779.

141   *Could I have conceived*   WGW, September 25, 1778.

141   *may excite others*   Schwartz, p. 35.

142   *I am now contrary*   Ellis, *Excellency*, pp. 285–86, n.

142   *an apathy*   Flexner, 4:310.

142   *Now, sir*   Woods, p. 42.

142   *chilled the air*   Ibid., p. 42.

142   *Mr. Stuart*   Ibid., p. 42.

142   *There were features*   Hannaford, p. 73.

142   *The distortion of the mouth*   Flexner, 4:312.

143   *I must entreat*   PGW, January 3, 1784.

143   *I am so hackneyed*   Ibid., May 16, 1785.

144   *the irksomeness* and *I have resolved*   Ibid., July 3, 1792.

144   *some little deviation*   Brookhiser, p. 127.

Chapter 9: Myth

146   *sanding down the rough edges*   Ibid., p. 154.

146   *long rhetorical flights*   Leary, p. 12.

147   *to show that* and *1 his Veneration*   Weems, *Washington*, p. xv.

147   *To this day*   Ibid., p. 6.

147   *As he spoke*   Ibid., p. 120.

148   *the Father of the Father*   Ibid., p. xxxvi.

148   *When George*   Ibid., p. 12.

149   *Yes, Pa* and *I want, my son*   Ibid., p. 14.

150   *Perhaps it was at that moment*   Ibid., p. 16.

150   *The story of the hatchet*   Ibid., p. xxiii.

150   *Is it not fair*   Mosher, p. 7.

151   *While it has become customary*   Bayley, p. 3.

151   *Stories about George Washington*   Weems, *Washington*, p. xxiii.

151   *grotesque and imaginary stories*   Ibid., p. xxiv.

151   *pernicious drivel*   Ibid., p. xxiv.

151   *a gap that Parson Weems*   Ibid., p. xxiv.

152   *As to his physiognomy*   Weems, *Franklin*, p. 1.

152   *lives among the clouds*   Ibid., p. 239.

152   *Writers who procure Reputation*   AFP, April 20, 1763.

153   *It makes human nature better*   Goodwin, Doris Kearns, p. 152.

153   *Wirt seems to have adopted*   Meade, p. 49.

153   *Like Weems*   Ibid., p. 50.

153   *was, indeed, a mere child*   Wirt, p. 25.

154   *genuinely admired his subject*   Elson, p. 8.

154   *His was a spirit*   Wirt, p. 137.

154   *irksome labor*   Elson, p. 8.

154   *is a practicing lawyer*   Wirt, pp. xiii–xiv.

154   *scanty and meager*   Ibid., p. xv.

155   *all the plaster of Paris*   Mayo, p. 6.

155   *I cannot learn*   Wirt, pp. 23–24.

156   *no law of the state* and *he was blamed*   Ibid., p. 419.

157   *was so unexampled* and *considered him as bringing*   Wirt, p. 50.

157   *so little acquainted*   Ibid., p. 89.

157   *In his accumulation*   Ibid., p. 419.

157   *morals were strict*   Ibid., p. 418.

158   *a poor book*   Mayo, p. 9.

Chapter 10: A Simple Epitaph

163   *I look upon death*   PBF, August 21, 1784.

164   *When I see nothing annihilated*   Brands, pp. 657–58.

164   *Here is my creed*   PBF, March 9, 1790.

165   *The bells were muffled*   Van Doren, p. 789.

166   *I proposed to General Washington*   Ibid., p. 788.

167   *The body of B. Franklin*   Isaacson, p. 470.

Chapter 11: The Tombstone at Red Hill

170   *I have long learned*   LCSPH, August 20, 1796.

171   *He was very infirm*   Morgan, p. 421.

171   *If I am asked*   Meade, *Revolutionary*, p. 450.

172   *The sun has set*   Morgan, p. 423.

172   *Mr. Henry is not*   Meade, *Revolutionary*, p. 448.

172   *No, indeed, my friend*   Ibid.

173   *No man ever vaunted less*   Ibid., p. 437.

173   *As for boasting*   Meade, *Revolutionary*, p. 438.

173   *have the glory*   Ibid., June 3, 1776.

173   *that posterity should pronounce*   Ibid., May 20, 1776.

173   *Farewell, first-rate patriot*   Virginia Gazette, June 14, 1799.

Chapter 12: An Early Death

176   *When the transient circumstances*   WGW, August 28, 1788.

176   *I have a tender reliance*   Chernow, p. 707.

176   *I am a sinner*   Ibid., p. 707.

176   *barbarous custom*   Ibid., p. 708.

177   *the creator of American capitalism*   Ibid., p. 345.

177   *from the moment at which history*   Malone, *President*, pp. 428–29.

177   *Vice, folly, and villainy*   Ibid., p. 714.

177   *an exuberant genius*   Chernow, p. 5.

177   *reputation for honesty*   Randall, p. 381.

177   *an all-pervading ardor*   Brookhiser, *Hamilton*, p. 185.

178   *ambition is prevalent* and *grovelling*   WAH, November 11, 1769.

178   *the son of President Burr*   WAH, 7:852.

Chapter 13: The Tourist Attraction

181   *my long forsaken*   Flexner, *Anguish*, p. 339.

182   *in the calm lights*   Ibid.

182   *wide-eyed Europeans*   Vidal, p. 2.

183   *the General*   Ellis, *Excellency*, p. 266.

184   *Unless some one pops in*   PGW, July 31, 1797.

184   *an indulgent host*   Vidal, p. 2.

184   *I was the first*   Ellis, *Excellency*, p. 266.

184   *I had rather glide*   WGW, March 25, 1784.

185   *His memory will be adored*   Hannaford, p. 41.

184   *On his front*   Ibid., p. 60.

184   *The scene is closed*   Brookhiser, *Father*, p. 199.

Chapter 14: A Message to the Future

187   *was sometimes not sure*   Ellis, *Sphinx*, p. 232.

188   *Would you believe*   Grant, p. 443.

188   *The practice . . . of publishing*   AJL, February 2, 1817.

188   *gruff, short*   Grant, p. 443.

189   *I leave others to judge*   AJL, June 15, 1813.

189   *sincere wish*   JC, Washington ed., 6:455.

189   *I have ever found*   Ibid., 6:394.

190   *There is a ripeness*   AJL, August 1, 1816.

190   *He took stock*   Burstein, p. 10.

Chapter 15: John Adams Survives

193   *Thomas Jefferson survives*   McCullough, *Adams*, p. 646.

193   *Our machines have now been running*   AJL, July 5, 1814.

193   *I am sometimes afraid*   Ibid., July 16, 1814.

194   *Divine favor*   McCullough, *Adams*, p. 647.

194   *In the structure*   SE, p. 379.

194   *Adams and Jefferson*   Ibid., pp. 193–94.

195   *Gracious God!*   McCullough, *Adams*, p. 623.

195   *I wish I could lay*   Grant, p. 439.

196   *would probably derive*   Ellis, *Sage*, pp. 241–42.

197   *This stone*   McCullough, *Adams*, p. 649.

Epilogue: The Autograph of a Not-So-Famous Man

202   *In his person*   Goodrich, p. 454.

203   *Mr. Gwinnett bore*   Ibid., p. 453.

204   *In the disappointment*   Ibid., p. 454.

BIBLIOGRAPHY

Electronic Archives

AFP   *Adams Family Papers*
GWP   *The George Washington Papers at the Library of Congress*
JC   *Jefferson Cyclopedia*
JMP   *The James Madison Papers from the Library of Congress*
TJL   *Thomas Jefferson Letters, 1760–1826*

Collected Works

AJL   *The Adams-Jefferson Letters: The Complete Correspondence between Thomas Jefferson and Abigail and John Adams.* Edited by Lester J. Cappon. Boston: Massachusetts Historical Society, 1959.

DAJA   *The Diary and Autobiography of John Adams.* Edited by L. H. Butterfield et al. Boston: Massachusetts Historical Society, 1961.

FP   *The Federalist Papers.* Edited by Isaac Kramnick. New York: Penguin Classics, 1987.

LCSPH   *The Life, Correspondence, and Speeches of Patrick Henry.* Edited by William Wirt Henry. New York: Charles Scribner's Sons, 1891.

PAH   *The Papers of Alexander Hamilton.* Edited by Harold Syrett et al. New York: Columbia University Press, 1961.

PBF   *The Papers of Benjamin Franklin.* Edited by Leonard Labaree et al. New Haven, Conn.: Yale University Press, 1959.

PGW   *The Papers of George Washington*. Edited by Donald Jackson et al. Charlottesville: University of Virginia Press, 1977.

PJA   *The Papers of John Adams*. Edited by Robert Taylor et al. Boston: Massachusetts Historical Society, 1977.

SF   *The Spur of Fame: Dialogues of John Adams and Benjamin Rush, 1805–1813*. Edited by John A. Schutz and Douglass Adair. San Marino, Calif.: Huntington Library, 1966.

WAH   *The Works of Alexander Hamilton: Comprising His Correspondence, and His Political and Official Writings, Exclusive of the Federalist, Civil and Military*. Edited by John Church Hamilton. New York: J. F. Trow, 1850.

WGW   *The Writings of George Washington*. Edited by John Fitzpatrick. Washington, D.C.: U.S. Government Printing Office, 1931.

Books and Periodicals

Adair, Douglass. *Fame and the Founding Fathers*. New York: W. W. Norton, 1974.

Alexander, John K. *Samuel Adams: America's Revolutionary Politician.*

Lanham, Md.: Rowman & Littlefield, 2002.

Allan, Herbert S. *John Hancock: Patriot in Purple.* New York: Beechhurst Press, 1953.

Bailyn, Bernard. "Jefferson and the Ambiguities of Freedom." *Proceedings of the American Philosophical Society* 137, no. 4 (1993): 498–515.

Barratt, Carrie Rebora, and Ellen G. Miles. *Gilbert Stuart.* Catalog of exhibit at the Metropolitan Museum of Art, New York. New Haven, Conn.: Yale University Press, 2004.

Beeman, Richard R. *Patrick Henry: A Biography*. New York: McGraw-Hill, 1977.

Boorstin, Daniel J. *The Americans: The Colonial Experience*. Norwalk, Conn.: Easton Press, 1987.

———. *The Americans: The National Experience*. Norwalk, Conn.: Easton Press, 1992.

Brands, H. W. *The First American: The Life and Times of Benjamin Franklin.* New York: Doubleday, 2000.

Brant, Irving. *James Madison: Father of the Constitution, 1787–1800.* Indianapolis: Bobbs-Merrill, 1950.

———. *James Madison: The Nationalist, 1780–1787.* Indianapolis. Bobbs Merrill, 1948.

Braudy, Leo. *The Frenzy of Renown: Fame and Its History.* New York: Oxford University Press, 1986.

Brodie, Fawn M. *Thomas Jefferson: An Intimate History.* New York: W. W. Norton, 1974.

Brookhiser, Richard. *Alexander Hamilton: American.* New York: Free Press, 1999.

———. *Founding Father: Rediscovering George Washington.* New York: Free Press, 1996.

Brooks, Jerome E. *The Mighty Leaf: Tobacco Through the Centuries.* Boston: Little, Brown, 1952.

Burns, Eric. *The Smoke of the Gods: A Social History of Tobacco.* Philadelphia: Temple University Press, 2006.

———. *The Spirits of America: A Social History of Alcohol.* Philadelphia: Temple University Press, 2003.

Burstein, Andrew. *Jefferson's Secrets: Death and Desire at Monticello.* New York: Basic Books, 2005.

Carlyle, Thomas. *On Heroes, Hero-Worship and the Heroic in History.* Lincoln: University of Nebraska Press, 1966.

Carpenter, Humphrey. *Geniuses Together: American Writers in Paris in the 1920s.* London: Unwin Hyman, 1987.

Cooper, Helen A. *John Trumbull: The Hand and Spirit of a Painter.* New Haven, Conn.: Yale University Art Gallery, 1982.

Davis, Kenneth C. *Don't Know Much about History: Everything You Need to Know about American History but Never Learned.* New York: Crown, 1990.

Durant, Will, and Ariel Durant. *Rousseau and Revolution:* Vol. 10 of *The Story of Civilization.* Norwalk, Conn.: Easton Press, 1992.

Ellis, Joseph J. *American Sphinx: The Character of Thomas Jefferson.* New York: Knopf, 1997.

———. *Founding Brothers: The Revolutionary Generation.* New York: Knopf, 2000.

———. *His Excellency: George Washington.* New York: Knopf, 2004.

———. *Passionate Sage: The Character and Legacy of John Adams.* New York: W. W. Norton, 1993.

Elson, James M., ed. *Patrick Henry and Thomas Jefferson.* Brookneal, Va.: Patrick Henry Memorial Foundation, 1997.

Everitt, Anthony. *Cicero: The Life and Times of Rome's Greatest Politician.* New York: Random House, 2001.

Fairholt, F. W. *Tobacco: Its History and Associations.* Detroit: Singing Tree Press, 1968.

Ferling, John. *A Leap in the Dark: The Struggle to Create the American Republic.* New York: Oxford University Press, 2003.

Flexner, James Thomas. *Anguish and Farewell, 1793–1799.* Boston: Little, Brown, 1972.

———. *George Washington and the New Nation, 1783–1793.* Boston: Little, Brown, 1970.

———. *George Washington in the American Revolution, 1775–1783.* Boston: Little, Brown, 1968.

———. *George Washington: The Forge of Experience, 1732–1775.* Boston: Little, Brown, 1965.

Franklin, Benjamin. *The Autobiography of Benjamin Franklin.* Norwalk, Conn.: Easton Press, 1976.

Garrett, Wendell D. "John Adams and the Limited Role of the Fine Arts." *Winterthur Portfolio* 1 (1964): 243–55. 1964.

Goodrich, Rev. Charles A. *Lives of the Signers to the Declaration of Independence.* New York: William Reed, 1829.

Goodwin, Doris Kearns. *Team of Rivals. The Political Genius of Abraham Lincoln*. New York: Simon & Schuster, 2006.

Goodwin, Lucia S., and James A. Bear Jr. "Edgehill Portrait of Thomas Jefferson, 1805–1982." *Monticello Keepsakes*, no. 29, 1982.

Grant, James. *John Adams: Party of One*. New York: Farrar, Straus and Giroux, 2005.

Haile, Edward Wright, ed. *Jamestown Narratives: Eyewitness Accounts of the Virginia Colony, The First Decade: 1607–1617*. Champlain, Va.: Round-House, 1998.

Harris, John. *Navigantium atque itinerantium bibliotheca: or, A compleat collection of voyages and travels: consisting of above four hundred of the most authentick writers . . . in the English, Latin, French, Italian, Spanish, Portuguese, German, or Dutch tongues*. London: T. Bennet, 1705.

Homer. *The Iliad*. Translated by Michael Reck. New York: HarperCollins, 1994.

Hughes-Hallett, Lucy. *Heroes: A History of Hero Worship*. New York: Knopf, 2005.

Isaacson, Walter. *Benjamin Franklin: An American Life*. New York: Simon & Schuster, 2003.

James, Clive. *Fame in the 20th Century*. New York: Random House, 1993.

Kagle, Steven Earle. "The Diary of John Adams and the Motive of Achievement." *Hartford Studies in Literature* 3, no. 3 (1971): 393–412.

King, Florence. *With Charity toward None: A Fond Look at Misanthropy*. New York: St. Martin's, 1992.

Kneebone, John T., J. Jefferson Looney, Brent Tarter, and Sandra Gioia Treadway, eds. *Dictionary of Virginia Biography*. Vol. I. Richmond: Library of Virginia, 1998.

Leary, Lewis. *The Book-Peddling Parson: An account of the Life and Works of Mason Locke Weems, Patriot, Pitchman, Author and Purveyor of Morality to the Citizenry of the Early United States of America*. Chapel Hill, N. C.: Algonquin, 1984.

Lind, Michael. "The Second Fall of Rome." *Wilson Quarterly* 24 (Winter 2000): 46–59.

Loveland, Anne C. *Emblem of Liberty: The Image of Lafayette in the American Mind.* Baton Rouge: Louisiana State University Press, 1971.

Malone, Dumas. *Jefferson and the Ordeal of Liberty: Jefferson and His Time.* Vol. 3. Boston: Little, Brown, 1962.

———. *Six.* Boston: Little, Brown, 1981.

Mayer, Henry. *A Son of Thunder: Patrick Henry and the American Republic.* New York: Franklin Watts, 1986.

Mayo, Bernard. *Myths and Men: Patrick Henry, George Washington, Thomas Jefferson.* Athens: University of Georgia Press, 1959.

McCullough, David. *John Adams.* New York: Simon & Schuster, 2001.

———. *1776.* New York: Simon & Schuster, 2005.

Meacham, Jon. *American Gospel: God, the Founding Fathers, and the Making of a Nation.* New York: Random House, 2006.

Meade, Robert Douthat. *Patrick Henry: Patriot in the Making.* Philadelphia: J. B. Lippincott, 1957.

———. *Patrick Henry: Practical Revolutionary.* Philadelphia: J. B. Lippincott, 1969.

Meschutt, David. "A Long-Lost Portrait of John Adams and an Unknown Portrait of Abigail Adams by James Sharples," *The American Art Journal* 32, nos. 1–2 (2001): 76–93.

Millard, Everett L. "The Browere Life Masks." *Art in America,* April 1950.

More, Sir Thomas. *The Utopia of Sir Thomas More.* Roslyn, N. Y.: Walter J. Black, 1947.

Morgan, Edmund S. *Benjamin Franklin.* New Haven, Conn.: Yale University Press, 2002.

Morgan, George. *The True Patrick Henry.* Philadelphia: J. B. Lippincott, 1907.

Mosher, O. W. Jr. "Parson Weems and That Cherry-Tree Story." *New York Times Magazine,* February 18, 1923.

Murray, Anne Wood. "George Washington's Apparel." *Antiques,* July 1980.

Nagel, Paul C. *John Quincy Adams: A Public Life, a Private Life.* New York: Knopf, 1997.

Oliver, Andrew. *Portraits of John and Abigail Adams*. Cambridge, Mass.: Belknap Press, 1967.

Peterson, Merrill D. *The Jefferson Image in the American Mind*. New York: Oxford University Press, 1960.

Randall, Willard Sterne. *Alexander Hamilton: A Life*. New York: Harper-Collins, 2003.

Rawson, Elizabeth. *Cicero: A Portrait*. Ithaca, N.Y.: Cornell University Press, 1975.

Renker, Elizabeth. "Declaration-Men and the Rhetoric of Self-Preservation." *Early American Literature* 24 (1989): 120–34.

Richard, Carl. J. *The Founders and the Classics: Greece, Rome, and the American Enlightenment*. Cambridge, Mass.: Harvard University Press, 1994.

Schlesinger, Arthur M. *The Birth of the Nation: A Portrait of the American People on the Eve of Independence*. New York: Knopf, 1969.

Schwartz, Barry. *George Washington: The Making of An American Symbol*. New York: Free Press, 1987.

Tebbel, John. *The Compact History of the American Newspaper*. New York: Hawthorn, 1969.

Tebbel, John, and Sarah Miles Watts. *The Press and the Presidency: From George Washington to Ronald Reagan*. New York: Oxford University Press, 1985.

Trumbull, John. *The Autobiography of Colonel John Trumbull: Patriot-Artist, 1756–1843*. Edited by Theodore Sizer. New Haven, Conn.: Yale University Press, 1958.

Tyler, Lyon Gardiner, ed. *Narratives of Early Virginia, 1606–1625*. New York: Charles Scribner's Sons, 1907.

Untermeyer, Louis, ed. *American Poetry from the Beginning to Whitman*. New York: Harcourt, Brace, 1931.

Van Doren, Carl. *Benjamin Franklin*. New York: Book-of-the-Month Club, 1980.

Vidal, Gore. *Inventing a Nation: Washington, Adams, Jefferson*. New Haven, Conn.: Yale University Press, 2003.

Weems, Mason L. *The Life of Benjamin Franklin; with Many Choice Anecdotes and Admirable Sayings of This Great Man, Never Before Published by Any of His Biographers.* Philadelphia: J. B. Lippincott, 1883.

———. *The Life of Washington.* Edited and introduced by Marcus Cunliffe. Cambridge, Mass.: Belknap Press, 1962.

Wills, Garry. *Cincinnatus: George Washington and the Enlightenment.* Garden City, N.Y.: Doubleday, 1984.

———. *James Madison.* New York: Times Books, 2002.

Wirt, William. *Sketches of the Life and Character of Patrick Henry.* Rev. ed. New York: Derby & Jackson, 1859.

Wood, Gordon S. *The Americanization of Benjamin Franklin.* New York: Penguin Press, 2004.

INDEX